BERNARD HÄRING

HOPE
IS THE REMEDY

 St Paul Publications

ST PAUL PUBLICATIONS
SLOUGH — ENGLAND

CONTENTS

PREFACE

It was a sociologist who, in January 1964, proposed the characteristic introduction to the Pastoral Constitution of the Church in the Modern World, *Gaudium et spes*, the joys and the hopes, the griefs and the anxieties of the men of this age. The years following the Council have provided ample evidence that 'hope' is the distinctive pass-word of the secular world and of the People of God in this era of rapid change, of illusions and disillusions. What the world expects from the People of God is above all a realistic message of hope, the courage to be and to live in the midst of the pangs of child-birth with a hope that gives new life.

The undreamed-of progress of modern science and technology have awakened new expectations which go beyond neoteric technical possibilities or scientific verification. They constitute a whole sensation of a flood-tide in progress and development, a sensation of hope in the total life style of a generation. The men of today keep a sharp look-out for totally new ways of investing their energies in the shaping of history and of their immediate environment, but in this new expectation, there are contingent forces of tension and frustration. After the destruction of two world wars, humanity hoped for peace; it is now shocked by the explosions of violence which rock their cherished dream.

The aggravation of the drug-addiction problem and the common awareness of the increasing environmental pollution are but two symbols of a new human experience of hopelessness and frustration. Man is confronted with new problems which are the results of his earlier hopes, better termed *illusions*.

9

Humanity is torn and shaken by the sensational hopes of yesterday and today wallows in anxiety neuroses.

In which direction will modern man react when his noblest hopes are destined to burial in this new age of anguish and neurosis while his capacity in the technological fields and in the pragmatic sciences seems to unfold at a geometric rate? Will he, in a kind of existential despair, invest all his energies in technology and its supporting sciences? The hippie movement seems to be a protest against such a decision. The hippies fear the emptiness of a world in which man's best efforts are expended for external progress while man as man has renounced growth. In final analysis, is not radicalism of this kind of protest a sign that mankind never renounces the hope of becoming more humane? By itself, is not the hippie protest an indication that man will abandon many other hopes in favour of his most existential longing? However, christian hope inspires a more healthy protest and a more effective remedy.

The renewal efforts in the Church, the ecumenical, biblical and liturgical movements, the awakening of the laity to responsible service in the Church and society, the ideas Pope John embodied so uniquely and the courage of Vatican II to set out into an uncertain future, were they not for many of us more than a sensation of hope? They represented more than we had dared hope to see in our lifetime. As a response, many realize that we can render thanks and honour God only by hoping for still greater things.

These well-founded hopes, grounded in the visible signs of God's gracious presence, are all the tones of hope in modern man. At the very core of man's life, there is a tension produced between the hopes of one particular field of endeavour and the danger of despair in other perhaps more important tasks, in the imbalance between the new experience of power on the one hand and the greater awareness of human limitations and frustrations on the other. Much sand was thrown into the mill of renewal by the very mixture of hope and by the impatience with which the technical man of today wanted to construct things which cannot take on the same rhythm as technological progress. Large bodies move slowly and the Church is no exception to this physical law; the result, therefore, is disillusionment and discontent perceptible in many parts of the world.

One reaction to this situation within the Church is similar to that of the hippies, namely, the innumerable underground churches which have sprung up in all parts of the world. In them are mirrored the many-faceted hopes and illusions of modern man. Unfortunately, the label of 'underground churches' is also affixed to sound groups that breathe spontaneity and endurance in creative suffering while others are no more than a grumbling church in sterile reaction against disgruntled reactionaries. It is my conviction, however, that on the whole, creativity as an effective sign of hope prevails.

At first glance, it may seem that at times, pessimism is more prevalent than hope. There are two very different and opposing groups that promote this mistaken impression. One need only scan the reactions to Pope Paul's utterances, decisions and actions. Even when, on the whole, his message is an appeal to courage and trust, there are cynics who quote only the expressions of concern, grief and despair; they are attuned to the pessimistic overtones only. It may be that these people need a scape-goat for their own anguish and lack of courage to face up to reality. They are angry because history has not set its seal on their hopes. The reforms they wanted and the speed they had opted for failed to materialize.

Others have dwelt on the pessimistic undertones of the Papal pronouncements because of their masochistic tendencies and their need to dwell in gloom and despair. They feel entitled to canonize their anxiety neurosis. The existential fear prompting their despondency is their futile search for liberation from the duty of committing themselves to salvific change.

All Christians must remember that these two vocal groups are not representative of the whole world or of the whole Church. Hope is not dead; on the contrary, hope is finding new classical expressions of which I will mention just two examples. The astronauts, who with almost incredible skill and courage, have opened new vistas on technological progress and human valour, in the midst of their successful exploits proclaimed to

11

the whole of mankind their praise of the Creator. It was a new awareness of the continued presence of God in the on-going creation. A similar example lies in the pilgrimages of Paul VI with his undaunted courage to by-pass all traditions and to visit twice in the Orient the leader of the Orthodox Churches before inviting him to a visit in Rome. Whatever may be said critically about the journeys of the Pope, are they not symbolic of the pilgrim Church setting out for new horizons in constant hope?

Also strongly indicative of hope are the results of the most comprehensive survey in religious sociology which was conducted in West Germany in preparation for the great Pastoral Council. Very interesting insights were yielded as to the prevailing anxieties, concerns and hopes. 4,400,000 Germans filled in the questionnaire. Striking was the fact that personal concerns and anxieties were very secondary. 44.2% expressed some worry over the uncertainty of the future of mankind and of their own future as opposed to 66.9% who indicated concern for peace as predominant. The 44.2% quoted above were included in the 55.1% who expressed personal uneasiness that after all our technological advances, a considerable segment of humanity suffers from starvation and poverty. 44.6% were worried about the difficulty of dialogue between the older and younger generations. Taken together, these concerns fail to meet the diagnostic requirements of an anxiety neurosis. On the contrary, they are healthy signs of a responsible attitude in view of the great tasks of humanity.

For only about 20.4% was the ecumenical movement with all its attendant changes any source of anxiety; the great majority approved the ecumenical opening of the Catholic Church. 46.4% clearly expressed the conviction that the Catholic Church should be even more daring and courageous in striving towards Christian unity.

When asked about the tasks of the Church, only a relatively small percentage gave preference to what would smack of religious individualism. The great majority of respondents expected the Church to be a prophetic voice in the world for social justice and the development of peoples, while not neglecting the religious task of honouring and praising God, of proclaiming salvation. The overall picture is indicative of a people searching for an integrated hope.

One is justified in asking: how representative was the 4,400,000 sample in relation to the 21,000,000 to whom the questionnaire was distributed? Admittedly, the group of regular church-goers was over-represented. It was therefore deemed advisable to sample for realistic representativeness of the West German population. The picture which emerged was essentially the same; however, it seems that among the regular church-goers and those admitting a positive rapport with the Church, hope and social concern figured more prominently.

Out of the conviction that hope is a great existential theme of this decade, I accepted primarily, over the last two years, those invitations for lectures and conferences that focused on the topic of hope. The ensuing discussions helped me to grasp better the complex reality. The book which I now present to the public emanated mainly from a workshop I conducted for more than 700 religious teachers: laymen, priests and religious, at Holy Name College in Oakland, California, in August, 1970, and the lecture series I gave at the International Catechetical Institute in London, Ontario, in September, 1970. I decided on publication because of the insistent appeals of the participants. However, I would never have found time and courage to do so without the most generous collaboration of Sister Gabrielle L. Jean. She offered a good part of her sabbatical year to transcribe the lectures from tape, to edit and re-edit them after our common reflection. I wish to express to her my profound gratitude.

Bernard Häring, C.Ss.R.

December 10, 1970
    Rome

Chapter 1

UNMASKING THE ENEMY

The science of catechetics has to explore a great variety of literary genres and since catechists are generally involved in a process of demythologization, I would like to begin with a myth or legend involving skunks. The very nature of the narrative reveals its imaginary character; nevertheless, it conveys a truth likely to be confirmed in the light of your own personal experiences.

Towards the end of the Council, I had a "vision" in which my olfactory sense came prominently into play. Before me was a great assembly, the Universal Congress of Skunks. Presiding at the opening session was the Supervisor of Devils, the Super-Skunk, who addressed his fellow-skunks in the following manner:

Dearly beloved and truly abominable skunks,

Over the past few months and years, you have been doing very poorly in terms of stinking and radiating frustration around you. You seem unable to cope with the challenge of that old guy, John XXIII, who could have died some years earlier instead of spreading optimism over the world contaminating even the secular segment and people outside his fold. But now, dearly beloved and equally hated devils, the Grand Council is proposing a new unified strategy the goal of which is nothing less than the transformation of the

15

Church, our enemy, into a perfect sacrament of pessimism, a truly visible and effective sign of our infernal odour. For this task, muster into service whatever grey matter you have at your disposal. Learn from modern psychology that there are no longer specific heresies to counter nor well-defined fears; use the persuasive force of anxiety. Anguish and anxiety must prevail: an anguished Pope, apprehensive bishops, anxious religious superiors, over-concerned liberals, anxious theologians, worried canonists—ANXIETY and ANGUISH are now the passwords; let anguish be a universal phenomenon.

The second part of our strategy pertains to the proper mixture of ingredients. The American chemists have much to teach us about our prized totem; they combine our skunk extract with other elements as a basic ingredient which gives perfumes a quality of permanence, the kind much coveted by sophisticated ladies desirous of flowery fragrance.

So far, you Stupid Devils have offered the world nothing but naked pessimism; it is no longer a marketable good. You must concoct a more effective mixture as suggested by today's chemists. Do not fear to speak out with unctious piety, with more concern for orthodoxy and progress, but include always 'skunk extract' as the basic element. Use it in such a way that there remains detectable in the final product our infernal odour of pessimism. Try it in all forms and combinations. No longer will you need to resort to violent attacks on God and religion; try the God-is-dead theology as one tactic. For those who claim He is living in the shrine of unchanging words, formulas and rituals, it is of utmost importance that you carefully and effectively deliver the message that God has died and will never rise again. Encourage them to talk about the hopeless absence of God on the one hand and make a concerted effort to speak to the people of God in a dead language; the outcome will be the same.

Inspire prominent churchmen to focus their interests and to spend all their energies on those truths which are irrelevant to us, for instance, the number of choirs of angels, whether angels are purely material or spiritual beings or both. Help them escape from their narrow world into lofty ideas, speculations and ideals. Keep them involved in lengthy theoretical arguments and hypothetical situations but manage to keep them away from any concern related to such foolish things as love and justice in the world.

Using all your gifts of oratory, preach faith, but let it be a faith without hope, consisting of formulas, a catalogue of things to believe; that will be one of our new gimmicks. Let them fight tooth and nail about "transubstantiation" or any other word far removed from the interests of the people. Help them properly translate their concern for authority in the Church as "those who take the place of God;" what better way is there of successfully driving God out of the world? When these people are cardinals, bishops or religious superiors, there seems to be no better way to maneuver God out of the world. Arouse their anger if someone resists them or holds a view of natural law or an opinion which differs from theirs. Let them suspend, silence or "transfer" those many priests who display sensitivity to the people's needs. Allow them to cry out: "My authority! What I say is God's word." Then confuse the people by saying that this is the Magisterium. Assist those brave cardinals who wish to define salvation by prescribing styles of dress for religious women. Whet the interest of all the people of God, lay, religious and cleric, in progress; incite them to impatience if progress does not come; make them angry and bitter.

Give considerable attention to the progressives, encouraging them to use at least ninety per cent of their energies fighting the conservatives, be they bishops, theologians, canonists, nuns or other holy people. Teach everybody to pray: "Sacred Heart of Jesus, trust in me!" Preach to the believers to have faith in themselves, and have them forget the grace of God which is a dangerous concept for us. Therefore, rally such strong believers; have them believe in their miracles. Suggest that they use drugs if needed to produce such visions, apparitions and wonders. Make sure that their miracles in

17

no way resemble those performed by our Enemy, Jesus, who relieved the poor, cured the sick and fed the hungry; such tendencies must be eliminated.

Single out for greater attention all the marginal religious interests you can think of, such as Churches arguing among themselves about the validity of certain successful marriages. Let pastors teach and stress that only those marriages are sacraments, are valid, which are performed with the prescribed ceremonies and meet the Church laws. Fan the flames of discussion on these matters; this tactic will free pastors from concerns relative to stabilizing marriages or educating spouses to that love our Enemy has taught. Then, beloved and stinking friends, tell them more about freedom; that is our business. We have to bring to the world the notions of self-determination and self-fulfilment. Each person must focus on his own freedom and become oblivious of the freedom of others. If this freedom is not imminent, let them indulge in self-pity and in anger. Present your proposals with very pious and attractive lures, with good faith and religiousness but keep the fundamental thrust of pessimism.

Do not relent in your efforts to preserve the Latin language and similar archaic tokens; adopt *Una Voce* as your battlecry. Be especially careful that the formulas for prayer remain always and everywhere the same. Encourage the pious people to pray and pray, hours on end but only with the old formulas, trusting that they will be all the more effective if they are duly counted and recorded. With others, you will have to teach them how to get God to do their will. If indulgences hold no more attraction for them, then teach them self-indulgence, self-pity and similar forms of secular prayer.

Blind the people to the merits of their opponents. The conservatives must call the liberals "hopeless cases" and the older folks must do the same with youth. Teach equally the conservatives, the regressives, the progressives, the liberals how to fight for progress, for Church renewal; what is most important is that they oppose and attack one another mercilessly.

Present the Church as a case of institutionalized criticism but keep constructive ideas out of the business. Suggest only sharp censorship to your adherents: criticism of the Church, of priests, of those who are ruling as well as those who come under them. Do not allow people to believe that "totem hunting" is dead. Inform them that the totem hunters were warriors who introduced all forms of aggressiveness into the world. Now the time is ripe for more totem hunting: critics criticizing critics, one group disparaging the other.

Let priests and nuns talk day and night about optional celibacy, but rightly understood as optional fidelity. Help them bring about the Association for Pastoral Renewal with its stated goal: to reveal to the whole world how miserably frustrated priests can be when they are expected to keep their promises. Make a great show of conservatives whose charism is to frustrate progressives. Incite the progressives to greater effort in radiating bitterness on those already frustrated by reforms. In all this be shameless; subsume all your activities under the caption of religion or faith or piety; you will then have a potent mixture.

Piously insist on the observance of all the commandments, save that of love and mercy. In the past, you did marvelously well with rigorism and Jansenism but this day and age calls for a new approach. Be wary of any method calling for love and concern for other people. Be voluble about Christian hope but avoid any mention of Christ's death and resurrection as a condition of hope. Never bring into play such old-fashioned notions as self-denial; speak only of an easy hope, a man-made hope, a secular hope for earthly progress.

Do not tolerate a sense of humour for it is related to humility and that could be fatal; present it only as a waste of time. Let your whole effort rest on a futile optimism built upon secular achievements or magic piety. You will then surely enlist others into our sect of pessimism.

19

Remember that our goal is to transform the Church of our enemy into a sacrament of pessimism. Therefore, on the desk of the Pope place daily the long list of sad events for his information; do the same with bishops, religious superiors, with everyone now outside our group. Be fearless in combining the various pious elements provided you include the basic and most potent ingredient of stinking pessimism.

The Supervisor of Devils rambled on for some time yet; at the end of the great oration, all the grown skunks said a pious "Amen!" and set out determinedly to implement the new unified strategy.

Are we post-conciliar Christians to be victims of this demonic strategy or can we say a firm "No! Begone Satan!"? It no longer matters whether one wears the label of conservative or liberal; what truly matters is that we place our trust in Christ, that we be men and women filled with divine hope and not with trust in ourselves.

Chapter 2

CHRIST OUR HOPE

Teilhard de Chardin liked to repeat: "The world belongs to those who offer it the greater hope." What is offered to us and what we can offer to the created universe is Christ, our Hope. As long as we do not present Him to the world by our witness of faith, hope and love, there will be others promising it greater hope. In our theological thinking as well as in our catechetical endeavours and in our lives, we should be most careful that nothing take the place of Christ nor conceal Him who is truly our Hope, our peace and our joy.

After first accepting Christ for ourselves, our concern has to focus on offering to the world the real Christ, the One who was, who is and who will be. There are too many caricatures of a sweet Jesus who disturbed no one, of the Jesus of a Social Gospel limited to this worldly life. As Christians, our mission is to present Jesus as He offered Himself to the world, as Christ, our Saviour and our Hope.

Christ is our Hope and the fulfilment of God's saving love, of God's saving mercy and of God's saving justice. He is our Hope as the great sacrament, the *great visible sign of God's fidelity* and love for all men. Christ is our Hope as the victor over all the power of frustration, over sin, over our solidarity in sinfulness and selfishness, over anguish and over death. Christ is our Hope as the risen Lord; He is the new creation. He is the final Word of God to man, the last and final prophet

21

promised to those who believe in Him and are truly His disciples.

Jesus is the great and ever present reality in which our common history was and is completely anticipated in a personal event. In Him are fulfilled all the past promises. All that was right, just and good in the times before Christ's incarnation, death and resurrection, was already inspired by His grace, preparing His coming in the flesh of this world, His death, resurrection, ascension and the mission of the Spirit who renews heart and mind, and the face of the earth. All that which throughout the ages is done with His grace bears the promise that He will complete the work in this history and beyond it. "The raising of Jesus to the status of Lord is a saving act of God which, at one point, turned the history which ended in His death into a fulfilled history. That is why it touches our own terrestrial history. We are faced here with a real event which is embedded in history. . . . While the apocalyptic approach puts the eschaton at the end of the history of this world, Christianity has put it within history itself. . . . In the man Jesus the future of mankind has been revealed to us: the fulfilment of the life of Jesus himself, in both its individual and collective aspects." [1]

So Christ who died for us and was raised for us is a real event in human history. Yet, this is more than just a past historical event; it is an event that gives meaning and direction to all our hope, to all past and future history. The final hope is already with us in Christ and through our faith in Him. This is our understanding of hope in terms of Christian existentialism. The Christian community that centres on "Christ is with us" is en route with the pilgrim Church that trusts in Him. However, Christ is also present as Judgment that is already going on in the world. Only if we accept Him also as Judge over the sinful world, over our selfish desires and the anguish caused by self-concern and self-pity, only then do we truly receive Him as the Saviour, our Hope.

---

[1] E. Schillebeeckx, O.P., "Some Thoughts on the Interpretation of Eschatology," *Concilium*, N. 41 (January, 1969), 54.

Christ is *our hope through faith,* but faith conceived as an absolute readiness to listen to Him, to treasure up His words in our heart, meditating and acting upon them. It is faith understood as a joyous, grateful acceptance of the One who is our Saviour, our Hope. It is through faith that we, His people, entrust ourselves to Him. We can then hope everything from Him, not in the manner of the ancient rabbi who asked, "How do I get God to do my will?" but rather according to the response he received from the greater rabbi in the Talmud: "Entrust yourself to God; conform your will to God's will and then God will do your will." Hope, then, is a very existential act; it implies entrusting ourselves to God in whatever He sends us, even unexpectedly; thus we trust that He is with us as our Saviour, as our Hope.

Christ is our Hope if we are willing to become with Him and in Him *promoters of hope,* symbols of promise, instruments of peace, signs of the Shalom, of the peace that has come in Him. He is our Hope if we entrust ourselves to Him for then we can conquer with Him the powers of evil and the great sins of despair, pessimism, anguish, self-centredness and self-indulgence.

Accepting Christ as our Hope means that with Him we can even *face death as a saving sign.* With Him, the condemned One, we utter the final word of trust: "Father, into thy hands I commit my spirit." If we have received the sacraments of hope after having lived accordingly and if we are conformed to Christ who has died for us and risen for us, we can claim that Christian optimism thoroughly discernible from that easy optimism suggested by the Supervisor of Devils. Christian optimism is at its best when daily labour, hard work, the difficulties of life, weakness, partial failure and contradiction assume new meaning in Christ, our Hope, who died for us.

Christ is our Hope by what He is, by what He says to us, by His life, by His death and resurrection. Therefore, the essential sign of Christian hope which distinguishes it so radically from all other forms of hope is the *Paschal Mystery.* Christian hope conquers the godless world, the alienated world, when in faith we say "yes" to God's will, the "yes" which consents to put to death our selfish desires. The sacraments are signs of hope if, through living faith, they are not just magic formulas but existential events, if they open our heart and mind and will, our whole life, our persons and our communities to the Paschal event of death and resurrection. Their reception, then, is a total opening and surrender to Christ, our Hope, so that we may become ever more visibly and effectively signs of hope for the world.

It will prove helpful to study some of the biblical texts on hope, especially the New Testament, in the one perspective of hope. It is the great book on hope; we turn, for instance, to the Epistle to the Romans for that optimistic outlook on salvation. Some of the mighty men of the past have invented many theories of pessimism, one of the most terrible being the eternal pessimism of limbo; billions and billions of innocent children who, without any guilt, would have been accommodated there, forever excluded from the vision of God. So the misdeeds, the wrongdoing of Adam would have been out of proportion with the salvation in Christ. "God's act of grace is out of proportion to Adam's wrongdoing." We have to test each theory against the background of the biblical teaching.

"God's act of grace is out of proportion to Adam's wrongdoing. For if the wrongdoing of one man brought death upon so many, its effect is vastly exceeded by the grace of God and the gift that came to so many by the grace of the one man, Jesus Christ. And again, the gift of God is not to be compared in its effect with that one man's sin; for the judicial action, following upon the one offence, issued in a verdict of condemnation, but the act of grace, following upon so many misdeeds, issues in a verdict of acquittal. For if by the wrongdoing of that one man death established its reign, through a single sinner, much more shall those who receive in far greater measure God's grace and his gift of righteousness live and reign through the One man, Jesus Christ" (Rom 5:15-17). The whole theology of St. Paul is a hymn of praise for God's grace. "It follows, then, that as the issue of one misdeed was condemnation for all men, so the issue of one just act is acquittal and life for all men. For as through the disobedience of the one man many were made

24

sinners, so through the obedience of the one man many will be made righteous" (Rom 5:18-19).

This hope is not offered to man magically. If the sinfulness of Adam is a fate we cannot escape, each can be freed in Christ but only if we accept Christ as He is, as the Father revealed Him, *Christ as the bearer of the burdens of all men.* We have to restore to the Christian sacraments, the sacraments of faith, the full character of hope, namely, that of entrusting ourselves to the Father in the manner of Christ. St. Paul explains it well: "By baptism we were buried with Him, and lay dead, in order that, as Christ was raised from the dead in the splendour of the Father, so also we might set our feet upon the new path of life" (Rom 6:4). So it is through God's precious offer, through God's commitment to us, through the fulfilment of His promises to us that we set our feet upon the new path of life by living according to faith and grace.

Christian hope is a gift, an *undeserved gift of peace,* but it is also a call to decision, to a total life of decision. Christian hope means then, that in Christ, by entrusting ourselves to Him, we can courageously face evil, accept our own need of *further conversion,* the lovelessness of others and all the investment of sin in the world around us and in our own heritage. We can face death just as we can face the mammoth task before us which, as St. Paul explains, is putting "to death our selfish desires". For this to become possible we need to entrust ourselves to Christ. We must be determined to take on the sentiments of Christ, his own outlook, the whole way he paved for us in selfless concern for others.

Let us return once more to the idea which is often omitted in a superficial theology and psychology of hope, to wit, that judgment is already going on. Those who insist on selfishly seeking themselves, those who want only to save their own lives are wasting their true selves, are losing their lives, are radiating frustration, are falling over and over again into the captivity of sadness and misery. Judgment is going on for those who place their trust in themselves, thus making themselves the centre of life instead of Christ, our Hope.

Christ is the saving Judgment if we recognize our faults, if we repent in readiness to do penance and to follow Him in hope and courage. The Epistle to the Romans, the great document on the genuine freedom of the children of God, gives us the direction. The law of the Spirit in Christ has rid us of the slavery of self-centredness, of the collectivity of sinfulness, of the law of sin and solidarity in sinfulness; it has freed us from the fear of a meaningless, hopeless death. "What the Law could never do, because our lower nature robbed it of all potency, God has done: by sending his own Son in a form like that of our own sinful nature, so that the commandment of the Law may find fulfilment in us, whose conduct, no longer under the control of our lower nature, is directed by the Spirit" (Rom 8:3-4).

Such is the theology of hope expressed in St. Paul. In one phrase, so many things are expressed: "our selfish self must be robbed of all its powers" because even with respect to the law of God which is spiritual, which is good, which is right, we can maintain a power-seeking attitude, a self-centred, self-protecting outlook. God has manifested the real outlook on the Law, that of redemptive love, by sending His Son in the form of a slave, the One who is to carry the burden of all his brothers in order to indicate that the selfish self is the way to perdition. As a sacrifice for sin, Christ has passed judgment and, therefore, man cannot be saved unless he accepts His judgment against sin in repentance, in sorrow and in readiness to amendment.

Christ is Saviour in accepting the conflict with the sinful world, particularly with the self-righteous world of the scribes and the Pharisees. He is a saving dissent for all, because He protests constantly against everything in us which is sinful and narrow. He does not spare his disciples the conflict with those who live on the level of the unredeemed man. By His whole life and especially by the Paschal Mystery, He teaches us that conflict can be a bearer of hope. For those who know Christ and entrust themselves to Him, all the growing pains and the polarization of our age become signs and stations of hope.

Hope is not only the greatest gift but also the greatest appeal. In hope our eyes are opened, our mind is cleared so that we may see the real commandment of God for unselfish Christ-like love. Only by entrusting ourselves to Christ and by accepting Him as our rule of conduct, the model of our life, we shall weaken our selfish self and become directed by the Spirit who is gift, anointment in joy, the giver of strength to serve our brethren.

Christian hope is based on a decision and imparts strength and meaning to our decisions. *God has decided to save us;* he has manifested the firm intention to save us provided, however, that we join in his promise, that we accept his great sign of hope, Christ, that we accept the Paschal Mystery as the decisive directive. St. Paul continues his hymn of salvation: "Those who live on the level of our lower nature have their outlook formed by it, and that spells death; but those who live on the level of the spirit have the spiritual outlook, and that is life and peace" (Rom 8:5-6). The spiritual outlook casts all our being, our desires and our decisions in the perspective of the Paschal Mystery, of Christ, the Messenger of peace and joy who makes Himself a ransom for all, who entrusts Himself in the final prayer on the cross: "Father into thy hands I commit my spirit." By the power of the Spirit He consecrates Himself for His brethren and thus honours His Father. Through the gift of the Holy Spirit, the disciples of Christ receive and gradually take on the outlook of the Paschal Mystery in death, life and peace. St. Paul states quite explicitly that there is no hope outside Christ and His spirit: "If a man does not possess the spirit of Christ he is no Christian" (Rom 8:9).

Christ is our Hope. It follows that hope is not just a teaching or a catalogue of things to look forward to, but it is *Christ in person.* Hope is incarnate. For Christ's disciples, it means a personal relationship. Men of hope are those who have firmly accepted Christ as their Saviour, as their brother and even as their servant. Hope implies a commitment to Christ, the Servant, in the service of our brethren. It is a new redeeming relationship to Christ with a totally new relationship to all things made in Him, to the whole creation and a new relationship with our brothers and sisters in the world around us. This is the existential meaning of a genuine theology of hope and of a meaningful catechesis. Both strive for the clearsightedness that will lead them to learn from what Christ said, from how He lived and died in order to urge His disciples to learn from Him the power of the gladdening news. Those who are chosen by Christ, and have chosen Him, our Hope, are living testimonies and instruments of hope for the world.

Chapter 3

HOPE AS DIALOGUE

Christian hope has a dialogical character in that it can be explained only in terms of interpersonal relationship. God first speaks to us, makes promises and fulfils them, shares with us His graciousness, which the Bible describes as His radiant countenance. This benevolence shines through all His works and deeds. Grace, then, is God's invitation to man for a personal relationship; man is honoured and he can communicate joy and peace if he is open to God's gift. The dialogical character entails a responsorial reality, namely, man's awareness, man's response to God's initiative in gratitude.

God's initiative precedes us in all life's events. We were first created without being consulted; then throughout our lifetime we are asked whether or not we want to accept God's design, to be really in His image and likeness. Our acceptance is indicated by our awareness of the One who created us. We were saved without being asked; again, it is God's initiative in grace, it is He who first offers us His promises, the pledge of His goodness. Our relatedness to Christ, our whole life, can be a response, but God's message, God's gift precedes our reply. We are open to and receive God's gracious gift if we entrust ourselves to Him gratefully.

Hope, then, is always an interpersonal relationship; it is a word that reaches man, a message that moves him, the Shalom that communicates its peace, but man is open, attentive, receptive and responsive. Christian hope does not arise from our own yearning or desire, from our own options; if our longing for beatitude has vital significance, a saving meaning, it is only because God has given it. In His benevolence, God offers us the fullness of hope in Jesus Christ. Through the Paschal Mystery Christ manifests and awakens hope; in our name, He gives the response of trust. This character of hope can never be stressed strongly enough. The initiative is God's own; He first manifests His goodness, kindness, promises, fidelity, and the work He has begun He will fulfil to the day of Christ's second coming.

Hope derives its dynamism from this personal relationship. If you reflect on the most fundamental relationship in the family, you have probably observed the difference between happy children who are loved, loving and trustful and their sad counterparts. Children reflect accurately what their parents' relationship is to them. If the parents wanted children, truly desired them and gratefully accepted them from God, these parents realize that they are blessed in their progeny. We see then that the eyes of the little ones and their whole being convey a feeling of hope and trust in their parents. If, however, the children are unwanted, if the parents constantly criticize and punish them, if they take no time to talk with them but maintain a domineering attitude towards them, then we find that the children mirror the parents' behaviour in their countenance and their whole being.

Similarly can the phenomenon of scrupulosity be explained in terms of interpersonal relationship. Any attempt to help a person so afflicted depends upon a true understanding of what it meant for the scrupulous person to have an authoritarian father who dominated fearful children and a frightened mother. The father concept of a policeman in the home has led to a distorted image of God the Father. Research in developmental psychology discloses that we tend to become trustworthy individuals when we are surrounded by trusting and loving persons. If one lives in the midst of hot-tempered people, malcontent and impatient individuals, one's behaviour will eventually be affected by them unless one consciously strives to counteract this influence through goodness, patience and kindness to the suffering people about.

In hope and despair, there is always an interpersonal relationship involved. In hope, we find two persons interacting and exchanging trust with an increasing readiness to respond to one another's needs. If in this perspective we grasp the notion that by nature man is made for hope, is yearning for beatitude, then we have already received a word of God. It is He who has "spoken out" man in this way; it is His creative word that makes man for hope. It follows that God never leaves man without hope. It is His creative word and as Christians we add that it is God's redemptive word that forever rescues man from sin which, in its fullest sense, is hopelessness. In his innermost being, man is called to hope because God creates so as to have sharers in His beatitude, sharers of His triune love. Man is what he is through the One who calls him so that he may become for others a sign of hope. Thus it is that God calls man in hope for hope, for beatitude, but it is a calling in freedom. Man can refuse to become a sign of hope for others; he then declines to became what he should be, what he could be; he will not come into his own, to the great hope in which he was called.

The whole of God's creation and redemption is a call to hope. Even when man sins, as in the case of Adam and Eve, God does not leave him without hope. There is not a text in the Bible where there is a mention of sin and judgment without a view of the hope to which God calls man. Even punishment sent by God is intended as the strongest final call for those who did not respond to the softer calls to hope. We find that it expresses God's holiness as in Prophet Hosea: "I will not turn round and destroy you; for I am God and not man, the Holy One in your midst" (Hosea 11:9). God's perfection is God's mercy and even in punishment He is the healer, He is calling to hope. It is of paramount importance in our catechesis and most particularly in our pastoral work that we never present a picture of sin alone because there exists no such thing in the Bible as a bare treatise on original sin; there is always a call to hope.

God it is who rescues man from the solidarity of sinfulness, from the slavery of sinfulness and who draws him to solidarity in hope. Christian hope, in the genuine redeeming sense, implies

31

a firm "yes" to the salvific plan of God. God created us to be sharers and concelebrants of His own beatitude; He manifests this intention finally and fully in Christ. Christ is both the great sacrament of God's promise, of God's calling to hope, and of man's response. Christian hope, then, lies in the firm "yes" of trust modelled on our Exemplar, Christ, who at the last moment responded to the Father's calling: "Father, into thy hands I commit my spirit" ((Luke 23:46).

It was customary for each Israelite to say every evening: "Into thy hands I commit my spirit." It becomes Christ's testament but He adds one word: "Father". There can be no greater "yes", no greater "amen" to God's promise, to God's calling to hope than the word of Christ: "Father, into thy hands I commit my spirit." Even Christ's last word is preceded by a message of hope for the brigand at His right: "I tell you this: today you shall be with me in Paradise" (Lk 23:43). It is His own trust and the entrusting of Himself to the Father that inspires the final trust, the final hope in all men. St. Paul masterfully expresses how Christ's trust in the Father and in His promises calls us and enables us to be men of hope. In his second Epistle to the Corinthians, we find: "The Son of God, Christ Jesus, proclaimed among you by us, was never a blend of Yes and No. With Him it was, and is, Yes. He is the Yes pronounced upon God's promises, upon every one of them. That is why, when we give glory to God, it is through Christ Jesus that we say 'Amen' " (II Cor 1:19-20).

The above text reminds me of an incident at the Council. In our drafting of the *Constitution on the Church in the Modern World*, we had used the words "Yes" and "Amen". One of the conservatives could not accept this modern language and pleaded with us to use the good, solid and well-established theological language. We had to inform him that we had simply taken the word of God!

"Yes" and "Amen" are basic concepts in the dialogue reported in the Bible, and Christ is the "Yes". Indeed, we can say that Christ is the incarnation of God's "Yes" to man, that after all our failures, all our sins, God's covenant remains firm. Christ is confirmed and anointed by the Spirit to be the fullest

32

testimony of trust and hope. He is the embodiment of God's salvific will, of God's saving presence. He is at the same time God's promise and man's hope through His full acceptance in our name. He is the Covenant, as the ancient Fathers of the Church used to say; in Him is the full representation for He stands for all. He makes visible in His own trust, in the way He entrusts Himself to the Father, that mankind can trust in God's merciful fidelity. Christ is the "Yes" and He speaks it in all his life. His life-blood seals the "Yes" of absolute trust and hope. He is the full visibility of God's undeserved grace, of God's graciousness. In Him the Father turns His countenance to us. He makes His design of hope fully manifest in the One who is the visible image of the invisible God. Christ is the explicit and attractive image of God's salvific will.

The character of hope arising from grace is a sign of the undeserved graciousness of God calling man to acknowledge, without security-insecurity complexes and without anguish, that he is unable by himself to build peace and trust or to repair the damage wrought by sin. He can then entrust himself to God in all his weakness, in all his sinfulness and with all his failures. This is a part of Christian hope. It is not a mysticism of sin that allows man to say: I can continue to sin because of the salvific plan of God to rescue man. On the contrary, this hope makes him similar to Christ; it awakens and frees all his energies for good. The starting point, the great perspective is one of grateful acceptance of the undeserved gift and the subsequent entrusting of oneself to God's graciousness.

Faith, hope and love all have this dialogical character. Where the responsorial aspect does not come through we find that man is still prisoner of his own ego. It is especially in prayer that man comes to the fullest awareness of this dialogical reality, to the fullest consciousness that it is God's own word, that it is God who first speaks to us; man is listening, opening himself, treasuring up the words, dwelling in the Word. But there is no possibility of abiding in the word, of letting the word dwell in us unless we are ready to give the full response, that of sharing our joy as instruments of hope. It is responsorial in that full sense of response, responsibility and co-responsibility.

33

The emphasis on the dialogical character of hope has inevitable consequences, for instance, in the grouping of the eschatological virtues which provide the full orchestration of hope. Leading all others should be gratitude. The origin of hope does not lie in man's futurology or any kind of utopia but in what God has already done for us. His promises come to us with His deeds, His gifts to humanity and to each individual. Gratitude should also be included for all that is worthwhile in tradition, that investment of goodness, of wisdom and justice in response to God's gifts and in cooperation with Him.

It is precisely at this point that my vision of hope differs in emphasis and approach from the theology of hope of Moltmann. He stresses the futurology of man and gives total attention to the open future. There is no doubt that hope looks forward to an ever greater future, to all that God's loving providence holds in store for us, but our expectations must be based on gratitude and thanksgiving for the very origin of hope. The guarantor of the open future is God Himself, His presence, all that He has already revealed and wrought in creation.

An undue emphasis on the future, especially when approached with a blend of utopia and scientific futurology could well favour a new Pelagianism and risk continuity even with respect to the vision of salvation history. When man makes his own dreams about the future and thus wants to take the future into his own hands, he is endangering that future. He will tend to pay too little attention to God's word and work as it comes to us throughout the history of salvation.

I am not intimating that hope should not give rise to a healthy imagination and phantasies about the future. On the contrary, the dynamic character of our age demands a strong emphasis on the open future, but it can be accomplished in praise of God who can and will do unprecedented new things. The good steward will always seek the happy balance between the "nova et vetera". One's grateful attention to the past can reach the here-and-now with its innate dynamism towards the future. It will ensure that wholesome equilibrium between continuity of life and courage in risk-taking.

Chapter 4

HOPE AS SOLIDARITY IN LOVE

Egotism is a hopeless existence in the deleterious collectivity of sinners, while hope is an initial liberation in solidarity in view of greater solidarity. Hope in solidarity means unity in genuine love.

In the first centuries, Christ was often spoken of as the Covenant. In Him, the Father offers the covenant to the whole of mankind and to all created realities. Christ, the radical representation of solidarity, offers Himself in the name of all men; the blood of the Redeemer becomes the law of solidarity since it is offered for all. It is thus the "blood of the new and everlasting covenant" offered for all. Christ is the sacrament of solidarity who makes evident in history that salvation is wrought in solidarity with Christ; He associates all men in His all-embracing love. He did not come to redeem isolated, separated souls; He came to redeem man in his wholeness: body, soul and spirit, in the wholeness of the person and the community, in the wholeness of man with the world about him.

A person is not a self-sufficient substance; one is truly a person in "being-with" the source of all personhood in heaven and on earth. Such is the reality God has revealed to us about His own personal life; the Father is by "being-with" his Son, by expressing himself in the Word, and the Holy Spirit is "being-with" in the Father and the Son. So the human person created to the image and likeness of the Triune God is not an isolated being; man is a gift of love spoken out by God's love.

In creating man to be a concelebrant of His love, God inserts him in a human family, prototype of community, for it is only in community that one finds trust and love. He can respond to the calling by living in responsibility and co-responsibility.

A human person comes to gradual self-realization through and for the community, by placing both capacities and things in common with others; there is a sharing of human experiences, reflections and co-reflections, of traditions, all the while retaining the capacity to reshape them for the common good. A person's life is one of co-responsibility in the sense that with others, together, we respond to Christ's rallying call. We come to our true selves, to our genuine individuality and unique name when responding to Christ who calls us together, who invites us to open ourselves to our brothers and sisters. Co-responsibility is always for the here-and-now in gratitude for the generations that have accumulated wisdom, the wealth of insights, experiences and reflections, in responsibility for the coming generations.

The world in which we live holds an accumulation of wrong-doing, of sinfulness, of selfishness, of oppressive power structures. This investment of sinfulness reflected in culture, traditions and collective prejudices is a source of temptation. However, as believers, we should first of all acknowledge gratefully that in our culture, in our environment is accumulated God's wisdom, goodness and justice; they have come to us through all the holy and righteous people who shared experiences, shared co-reflections in the common striving for goodness through thousands of generations. We have to face the reality that we are born into a world for which we are deeply indebted for so many good things, but that we are also tied up with a bad heritage, with a sinful environment.

Sin was first introduced into the world when man failed to respond fully to God's original design. God, the Creator, fashioned us for oneness, for solidarity; man was meant to share in co-responsibility. The Book of Genesis is more than a chronicle; it reveals God's original design: man and woman are made for each other, are equally created to the image and likeness of God and are joined together in the presence of God in mutual gratitude. The whole of mankind is prefigured in this mutual acceptance in the presence of the Creator. Then follows sin; Eve, alone with the serpent of her selfishness, desires freedom for herself, greater wisdom and more power. What happened in the great theological vision of the sacred author is that the communion with God or prayer was discontinued. Instead, there came the monologue, the self-seeking, and unavoidably there followed mutual contamination with solidarity in sinfulness which tradition calls "original sin".

When genuine solidarity breaks down, there arises solidarity in evil. Original sin, then, has started chronologically with one who could have done good but did not, who could have avoided evil but did not. However, it was not just one couple that burdened us with a bad heritage. We are all Adam and Eve, we invest in selfishness when we fail to do the good we are called to do, when we refuse to invest in goodness, kindness and gentleness in human history. The sacred author of Genesis makes it clear that Adam and Eve were not solely responsible for everything; agreed, they indulged in futile pursuits but their descendant, Cain, indulged in much greater sinfulness. Cain was not, chronologically, the first son of Adam for he could not have been a city builder. He is a son in the broad sense of being a descendant, but he represents those in whom sinfulness has come to a climax.

In Genesis again, there is mention of Lamech as the fourth descendant of Cain; sin has multiplied in Lamech. Lamech, a domineering polygamist, threatens his wives: "Wives of Lamech, mark what I say: I kill a man for wounding me, a young man for a blow. Cain may be avenged seven times, but Lamech seventy-seven" (Gen 4: 23-24). This is a biblical indication of how sin can multiply itself, but it must not necessarily be so. There is the family of Abel, replaced by Seth, where once again man began to adore God; sin was overcome at least to some extent.

So original sin is not just a replication by procreation as St. Augustine thought, nor is it a stain on the soul that can simply be washed away by baptism as stated in the Baltimore Catechism; original sin lies in that tremendous mystery of solidarity. God has made man for solidarity because He is the one Creator; His whole creative work manifests oneness, solidarity. However, man is called to solidarity in freedom; man enjoys the freedom to accept or to refuse solidarity in good. Should he refuse, he falls into a solidarity of evil, tied up with all the powers of selfishness, the powers of individualism, and he joins the company of domineering egotists.

The story of Joseph Stalin well illustrates the point. When a seminarian, Stalin had started a circle on Marxism. The fact was brought to the attention of the seminary authorities who soon dismissed him. Immediately, Stalin gave the seminary director the full list of names of all the students who had participated in the Marxist circle. Later in the course of his difficulties with Trotsky, someone reminded him that he had been a traitor from the very beginning to which he responded: "You are an idiot from beginning to end. If I had not given that list to the director, these cowards would have become coward priests. I forced them to stand together." This is solidarity in evil.

Stalin later organized the Communist party in Georgia, the southern part of Russia. He did not seek support for his organization from the poor; he collected money from the most wealthy people telling them quite bluntly: "You are paying for the Communist party", and each one was told how much he had to contribute. When anyone refused, he served notice that he and his men would return in two weeks at which time one would have to pay double. Many paid immediately; those who did not were harassed by fires on their property, explosions so that restoration and repairs became more costly. When Stalin and his friends returned, they received payment in full. Once he was caught on the spot by the police while extorting payment from a capitalist. The officer said: "Now we have proof." "Oh no," said Stalin, "it was my friend who forced me to accept this money." The intimidated capitalist then rescued Stalin by confirming his statement: "I forced him to accept the money." He was very concerned for his material possessions; he did not want to be burned out. Thus the capitalists were truly financing their own destruction. In my eyes, this historical fact magnificently illustrates the mystery of original sin, the accumulated power of individualism, of self-centredness; the more it is amassed the stronger the ties become. Finally, it is nothing other than hell where selfish people live in full solidarity of evil with other selfish people.

We must be ever mindful that it is not just Adam and Eve who got the sin-ball rolling, but all of us who fail to live for one another in genuine co-responsibility. Happily, God never left man without hope. There was still Abel building up goodness, offering a sacrifice of trust. There was always the genealogy of those who served God evincing the presence of God in man. Even Cain was marked by a sign of God's protection so that total self-destruction of sinners was avoided.

Finally, salvation becomes fully manifest in Christ who bears the burden of man. The tremendous sacramentality of solidarity in Christ is already forecast and partially revealed at the baptism of Jesus in the Jordan by John the Baptist. The ritual baptism of repentance was a very existential, prophetic anticipation of the baptism on the cross, the baptism in the blood of the Redeemer. Christ wanted to be baptized during the general baptism (Lk 3 : 21) where the "bad characters" came to John the Baptist to be cleansed in repentance. Christ thus manifested that His baptism is the liberation of all through the One who bears the burdens of others, His brethren. He intended that they too bear the burdens of each other (Gal 6 : 2). It is more than symbolic that Jesus was crucified surrounded by brigands and that He responded to the one who had come to appreciate the saving solidarity with Him: "I tell you this, today you shall be with me in paradise" (Luke 23 : 43). Christ is the embodiment, the incarnation of redeeming solidarity not only in the ritual celebration of baptism in the Jordan but in all His life and in His death. In terms of human history, it now means that each of us has to make a choice as to whether he wants to associate himself with Christ in saving solidarity and in hope or remain within the power of the sinful, deleterious solidarity. There is no other way out of original sin than by accepting existentially and wholeheartedly solidarity in Christ. Only then does baptism become the sign of salvation, the sacrament of hope in solidarity.

39

Such is the perspective needed for a better understanding of the most characteristic texts on solidarity. In his Epistle to the Ephesians (4:1-16), Paul writes: "I entreat you as a prisoner for the Lord's sake. As God has called you, live up to your calling. Be humble always and gentle and patient too. Be forbearing with one another and charitable. Spare no efforts to make fast with bonds of peace the unity which the Spirit gives." At the very heart of the theology of hope is the Holy Spirit in whom and through whom Christ is sent to the poor and is anointed to dedicate Himself for all. The mission of the Spirit through the risen Lord is a calling to spare no effort of hope in solidarity. "There is one body, one Spirit as there is also one hope held out in God's call to you." Here we see the great theological vision of Paul, the prisoner of Christ, totally given to the saving mystery of Christ in solidarity with all men and the whole creation, calling all to hope through this solidarity.

Paul is entreating the disciples of Christ to make fast with bonds of peace the unity which is the gift of the Holy Spirit. The Spirit himself is the bond of peace, the bond of unity in saving solidarity. "There is one body and one spirit as there is one hope." The body of Christ who is anointed by the one Spirit is the body given for all. Christ, the Anointed, gives His body and blood "for the life of the world" (Jn 6:51). In the Eucharist Christ unceasingly gives Himself for the life of the world and those who receive Him, not only physically but in faith and hope by the grace of the Spirit, will give themselves for the life of the world in the power of the same Holy Spirit.

The fourth chapter of the Epistle to the Ephesians leads to the culmination of hope: "There is one hope held out for you in God's call to you" (Eph 4:16). The truth of salvation and baptism reminds us that for the isolationist, for the individualist, for the egotist there is no hope. The one who wishes only to save his soul while remaining unconcerned for the world is, by necessity, lost because he is caught up in the deleterious solidarity. He loses his soul because there is only one hope which is solidarity with Christ.

The Church Fathers viewed Christ as the rallying call. The Catechism of the Council of Trent says: "Ecclesia, id est convocatio", the Church is the rallying call in Christ; we are called to hope in togetherness. St. Paul continues: "One Lord, one faith, one baptism; one God and Father of all, who is over all and through all and in all. But each of us has been given his gift, his due portion of Christ's bounty" (Eph 4:5-7). Each of us has received his own gifts but all in view of the Spirit, by the one Spirit, in view of the one Body of Christ, in the glory of the one Lord and the one baptism in the Spirit. This central truth of salvation obliges us to use our gifts in the service of all; otherwise, they are lost. Salvation in hope does not allow a fundamental motivation concentrating on self-fulfilment; hope is a matter of dedication, of consecration, of giving of oneself. God will then take care of our fulfilment. If we seek primarily self-enhancement in self-determination, then the powers of evil will take over and keep us in the deleterious solidarity of sin.

Paul then emphasizes the variety of God's gifts but always in view of solidarity. "And these were his gifts: some to be apostles, some prophets, some evangelists, some pastors and teachers, to equip God's people for work in His service, to the building up of the body of Christ. So shall we all at last attain to the unity inherent in our faith and our knowledge of the Son of God — to mature manhood, measured by nothing less than the full stature of Christ." All charisms and ministries are signs of hope for all if received and used in saving solidarity. "Let us speak the truth in love; so shall we fully grow up into Christ. He is the head and on him the whole body depends. Bonded and knit together by every constituent joint, the whole frame grows through the due activity of each part, and builds itself up in love." This chapter four of the Ephesians is a magnificent *leitmotiv* and programme of hope in solidarity and of solidarity in hope; there can be hope only in saving solidarity.

The Constitution on the Church in the Modern World focuses strongly on Christian personalism in all its dimensions of community and solidarity as suggested by the Pauline text. The Council Fathers reaffirmed their conviction that a person is not a being for himself. The human person finds his true self through his consecration for others, by "being-with" and for his neighbour in the service of the common good. Articles

11 and 12 very strongly emphasize the whole vision of the body of Christ as the Church, the community of love in solidarity. In Article 24, there is a classical formulation which can be summarized as: man cannot truly find himself except through a sincere gift of himself. The following article reads: "When the structure of affairs is flawed by the consequences of sin, man, already born with a bent towards evil, finds there new inducements to sin, which cannot be overcome without strenuous efforts and the assistance of grace" (GS, Art. 25). Article 72 gives an understanding of solidarity as a sign of the kingdom of God: "Whoever in obedience to Christ seeks first the kingdom of God will as a consequence receive a stronger and purer love for helping all his brothers and for perfecting the work of justice under the inspiration of charity."

The defeat of individualism turned out to be one of the important contributions of Vatican II. From the beginning to the very end, in all its decrees and its documents, there is this kind of personalism which is a "yes" to community; it is a "being-with", a commitment to, and it is freedom in the sense that one is liberated from selfishness to be consecrated by the Spirit to the service of all. The Spirit makes us the body of Christ who gives His body for the life of the world.

It is very important that in prayer, in personal motivation, in theology and in catechesis we return more and more to this vision of Christ: the absolute solidarity with all of mankind and indeed, with the whole of creation. He is the Saviour of the world in His body and blood; He is the calling to the new heaven and the new earth for fullness in solidarity. He is the saving sign of hope as the all-embracing sacrament of solidarity. He wants us to be witnesses of this hope in solidarity visibly and effectively, and through us, His disciples, He wants others to be consecrated to the same work.

Chapter 5

FAITH FOUNDED IN HOPE

Hope tests the mettle of our faith. A proper understanding of this truth leads us to grasp the inter-relatedness of faith, hope and love in perspective.

Hope is faith and love on pilgrimage; it is not something besides faith nor is it something apart from love. Hope is the internal dynamism of faith and love, an aspect poorly understood by a rationalistic and all too Hellenistic approach to faith. Faith was presented as a system of well-defined truths, as a catalogue of beliefs in an establishment theology too strongly influenced by Canon Law. There are abiding truths, it should not be denied, but only in the One and through the One who is the fullness of Truth. Our concepts are never the full truth; they are only in a pilgrim situation.

The Christian concept of faith in the Bible refers to trust in the Lord, the faithful One, who pledged to remain with mankind, gradually revealing Himself to us. Salvific faith lies in entrusting oneself to the One who reveals Himself as the Way, the Truth and the Life. It is trust in the Lord of history who was, is and will come, who is present in His work, in the continuous creation. Faith can be described in relation to salvation history of which we are part; it is a reality in which we are involved with God. In faith, the heart of the matter lies in the history of God with man in his world and the history of men with God in openness to God's revealing action.

43

According to dogmatic theology, revelation came to an end with the death of the last Apostle or with Christ, but this should not be misunderstood. Truly, Christ is the final Word; God will never give any greater word, message, comfort or truth to the world than Christ, because He is the Word Incarnate. He is the fullness of revelation, the centre of revelation. But Christ is still on the way of His final coming. He has revealed Himself once in His incarnation, life, death and resurrection but in view of His final coming in the Parousia. So revelation in Christ's life 1970 years ago does not bring history to an end but opens new horizons to history since Christ continues His work, His word, in an on-going revelation. To the end of history, man must pay attention to Christ's word if he is to come to an understanding of God's design: "My Father has never ceased his work, and I am working too" (John 5: 17). God's work is always illuminating, His words are trust-inspiring because they constitute a progressive unveiling of the total plan of God.

There is a very striking vision in the fifth chapter of the Book of Revelation about the book of history sealed with seven seals. The question arises in heaven: who can unseal the book? There is silence and expectation followed by a liberating response: the Lamb that is slaughtered and stands before the throne of God, "the Lion from the tribe of Judah, the Root of David has won the right to open the scroll and break its seven seals" (Rev 5: 5). The book is then unsealed but interestingly enough, nobody reads. There are events, the great happenings of history but understood in the light of Christ, understood as preparing His final coming; there are new events and thus a continuing message. So all of history is an ongoing revelation; it is not something apart from Christ, nor it is something in the sense of those who speak of a post-Christian era where things are better understood without Christ. That amounts to a denial of faith. It is in Christ, in view of Christ, through the gift of Christ, through the gift of the Holy Spirit, in the community of the faithful looking to Christ that history can be understood as a continuous revelation. The great Actor is the Word in whom all things were made and who has come to redeem history. Therefore, each event is also a word of the Word.

In the Hebrew language, the same word "dabar" means event and word, so that all the events of history, all the signs of revelation are a word, a message, a disclosure. All things are made in the Word, and there is not one thing that is not made in Him; He is the Word. Therefore, historical events have a character of revelation for those who look to Christ, for those who, through the Spirit of Christ are open-minded. For a Christian to become complacent to the point of asserting that he has known everything for a long time, that he knows all the answers, would mean total unfaithfulness to God disclosing His majesty, His wisdom, His salvific designs in the events and the ongoing endeavours of the community of believers. All events are to be seen in the light of Christ.

Salvation history and the whole of human history, past and current, are to be seen as an integral part of the Christian faith. Faith in Christ makes human history infinitely more interesting, more dynamic than philosophical systems, because it constantly manifests new horizons and introduces new perspectives. Therefore, faith calls for total openness to events, to all that God does and wills to do in human history, and summons us to trust in the Lord of history. Such openness includes praise for all the marvellous deeds He has done and for the most wonderful fact that He has revealed Himself in His servant and Son, Jesus Christ. Faith is this constant doxology, praise of God with the realization that events are encounters with a God infinitely greater than our words, our concepts, our theology can ever express. Through hope the believer is trustfully on the way with the God of history looking forward to His constant coming.

Faith includes a dynamism towards a better knowledge of God in ever greater love, in ever greater trust. This hope characteristic of faith is very strongly expressed in the Epistle to the Hebrews. "And what is faith? Faith gives substance to our hopes, and makes us certain of realities we do not see" (Heb 11: 1). Faith has essentially that dynamic character; its nature is hope, it gives assurance to our hopes because God does not reveal abstract ideas or a philosophy but trust-inspiring truths of salvation. In each age, He shows the way that leads onwards towards salvation.

"It is for their faith that men of old stand on record" (Heb 11:2). Paul then points out the hope structure of faith in the Patriarchs, in people who belonged to Israel and others who did not; he finds faith in them, in their openness to new events. "By faith, Abraham obeyed the call to go out to a land destined for himself and for his heirs, and left home without knowing where he was to go" (Heb 11:8). "By faith, Abraham, when the test came, offered up Isaac . . . for he reckoned that God had power even to raise from the dead" (Heb 11:17-19). "By faith, Moses left Egypt, and not because he feared the king's anger; for he was resolute, as one who saw the invisible God" (Heb 11:27).

Strikingly apparent is the hope character in Isaac's blessing and in the whole life of Joseph. "By faith, Isaac blessed Jacob and Esau and spoke of things to come. By faith Joseph, at the end of his life, spoke of the departure of Israel from Egypt, and instructed them what to do with his bones" (Heb 11:21-22). It is ironic that some religious congregations and theological schools have taken more care of the dead bones of their founders than of their spirit. They forgot the first part of the instructions, namely, the "departure" and so failed to see the challenge of hope in the "bones". Well indicated here is that not even dead bones should remain in the same place; even the bones should be moved, should depart.

"By faith Moses, when he grew up, refused to be called the son of Pharaoh's daughter, preferring to suffer hardship with the people of God rather than enjoy the transient pleasures of sin. He considered the stigma that rests on God's Anointed greater wealth than the treasures of Egypt" (Heb 11:26-27). This text stresses particularly the fact that salvific faith frees from every kind of security complex. It is evident that all the aforementioned had the same vision of faith as a dynamic structure, a readiness to look forward, to go through the newness of trying experiences with trust in the Lord of history. Through hope, faith is more closely related to events than to a set of formulated truths.

"And what of ourselves? With all these witnesses to faith around us like a cloud, we must throw off every encumbrance, every sin to which we cling, and run with resolution the race for which we are entered, our eyes fixed on Jesus, on whom faith depends from start to finish" (Heb 12: 1). So faith is setting out, as St. Paul insists, running the race, looking to what is ahead and forgetting what is behind (Phil 3: 12-14). Evidently, faith is not imprisoned in an establishment; this point should be made very clear to those people whose "faith" is shaken because answers which they had memorized so well from the Catechism are no longer repeated. Like the venerable grandfather in his old age, these are people who like to repeat the same stories of their younger days thinking they will be of interest to today's youth. This is an establishment concept of faith. Concepts and words have their context in history and when placed in a different historical period, they change their meaning. But through its hope structure, faith is altogether more than a well-defined set of fully explained concepts. Faith is a call of the Lord of history and a response of man to the challenging events of the history of salvation in the ongoing history relating man and God. Therefore, we should not be so shocked if we come only gradually to a better understanding of faith in its existential character; salvific faith is a trustful encounter with the God of history. Faith means one is on the road with Him. It is particularly in times of trial, in periods of transition and profound changes that God calls for a greater trust, for a more radical entrusting of ourselves to Him and for a more painstaking effort to understand the signs of the times.

Christian faith is so different from an ideology, from a philosophy or a system of thought. It is a daring earthly history of man with God towards the fullness of light and life. It is through the intrinsic dynamism of hope that faith turns us simultaneously to the here-and-now and towards the final fulfilment. Faith is life, a trustful life in the light of Jesus and in partial darkness because it is an encounter with a mystery which is always infinitely greater than man can grasp in his earthly life. St. Paul expressed it well in his first letter to the Corinthians: "Now we see only puzzling reflections in a mirror, but then we shall see face to face" (I Cor 13: 12). We must try to understand this more thoroughly; what we see, what our words express, what the catechism teaches us, what the theologians say: all taken together they are but a puzzling reflection. Woe to us if we feel we possess the truth totally, if we refuse to exert new efforts; for without the constant openness and unrelenting, trustful effort to grasp past events in the here-and-now and reaching out for the future, we have denied the mystery of faith. Faith never allows establishment, complacency or lazy repetition. Formulas repeated indefinitely are no longer the message of the living God of history. There must be a constant effort to appropriate them, to understand them more deeply in the context of the ongoing events which are disclosures of God's salvific plan and loving designs for us.

Faith can reach a profound firmness through unflagging hope and trust in the Lord of history, but with respect to the expression of the mystery of God and of His design, our faith is always of infinite imperfection. St. Thomas Aquinas explains it by "analogy" while conveying the meaning: it is similitude in an ever greater dissimilitude. What we see and are able to express now bears similitude with the event we hope for in the final fulfilment, but we should remember that this holds true in view of the ever greater dissimilitude of all our knowledge and achievements in comparison with God's total design. Faith filled with hope is truly the way manifesting the right direction if we are joining the pilgrim Church in her definitions, in her guidelines, in her preaching of the Gospel, but it is only a directive, a similitude that points in the right direction. It is not to be confused with Truth as it is in God and is to be made manifest at the day of fulfilment. Faith includes the constant call for growth, for greater depth, for clearer vision, for a broader perspective in total awareness of our limitations.

This vision was thoroughly discussed at the Council when the theologians of the Holy Office presented the draft on the two sources of revelation, namely, Bible and Tradition. For them, tradition seemed to be a library, books and very specifically, those books containing all the decision of the Holy Office and of the various Sacred Congregations. They were thoroughly mistaken in presenting faith almost as if it were a catalogue of things, a frozen tradition, an establishment. Faith confronts us with a torrent of life. Tradition is a living tradition with God keeping things going, keeping us alive, opening our eyes, arousing us from time to time, assisting the Church in her direction by not allowing the Church any self-complacency, and indulgence in formalism. It is a torrent of life, a live tradition through the presence of the living God in the ongoing history of salvation. Faith in Israel and in the Church of Christ is kept alive by the great prophets who shake the establishment when there is danger of the Church's falling into ritualism and formalism.

In the history of salvation, there is discontinuity because of our sins and there is a totally different but salvific discontinuity when God sends prophets, great saints like Pope John, manifesting more clearly that we cannot settle down, that we have to try to grasp more vitally the here-and-now in the light of the total tradition and in responsibility for the future. There are, then, two different discontinuities; one is based on our sins and the other is a discontinuity caused by God, ever faithful, who mercifully opens our eyes and gives us a new chance for a deeper conversion. It is very important that we hold the right concept of tradition, one that allows us to set out courageously on the saving way to the future but with trust in the living God. He is faithful to Himself while gradually manifesting ever new things which disclose His master design in absolute faithfulness.

The community of faith must never err by confining itself to the bare exploration of the Bible. The priests and the Pharisees, the scribes and the lawyers, the theologians and the canonists of Israel, all explored the Bible explaining each text and discussing each word but they were not open to the signs of the times, to the great presence of God in his servant and Son, Jesus Christ. They were only looking back to dead texts, to the written word, to lifeless formulas.

The Church as the bride of Christ is recognized by her openness to the signs of the times. The Council calls 'signs of the times' those cues to the salvific presence of God. For believers all events, particularly those concerning unity and brotherhood of man, are a call to openness. The Church as a community of faith is on pilgrimage with the Lord of history,

D

but she will never lose heart when confronted with new events and problems because she walks always with the same Lord Jesus Christ. Our epoch has to become more Christian, more Christ-like, that is, more aware of the faithfulness of Christ to Himself in all new events, aware of His urging all of us to live in today's context according to His love disclosed once and forever. He reveals Himself in the covenant with man in history and throughout history in view of His final coming. Faith, then, consists essentially in these two aspects: a grateful "yes" to what God has already done and manifested, but also a trustful openness and expectation to what He will do and reveal in vigilance for what He actually calls for here and now. Christian faith is an encounter of the total human person with the Lord of history revealing Himself and His design about history. It is only through trust and hope that the believer remains in salvific contact with the history of salvation.

Where God reveals Himself in His events through His Word that is acting, that is creative, He calls for a creative response. Faith then includes, of necessity, that we be ready to act on the word. I gave the title *Acting on the Word* to my book on the evangelical counsels because of its centrality in the Sermon on the Mount. Christ, after having revealed His salvific plan in the new law of the beatitudes, insists: "Not everyone who calls me 'Lord, Lord' will enter the kingdom of Heaven, but only those who do the will of my heavenly Father" (Matt 7:21). " 'What then of the man who hears these words of mine and acts upon them? He is like a man who had the sense to build his house on rock. The rain came down, the floods rose, the wind blew, and beat upon the house; but he did not fall, because its foundations were on rock. But what of the man who hears these words of mine and does not act upon them? He is like a man who was foolish enough to build his house on sand. The rain came down, the floods rose, the wind blew, and beat upon that house; down it fell with a great crash'. When Jesus had finished this discourse the people were astounded at his teaching; unlike their own teachers he taught with a note of authority" (Matt 7:24-29). Behind the word speaking in historical events is the great Event, the Creator, the Word, the Redeemer. Faith cannot be separated from the readiness to act upon the word according to the present opportunities.

Wherever faith is accepted only as a closed system of well-defined dogmas, of formulations, the dogma itself is misunderstood and such a faith loses its dynamic hope structure, loses contact with the living God and with the here-and-now. Salvific faith is a surrender to God Himself who reveals Himself, discloses His salvific intentions by acting, by a dynamic word, by an ongoing series of events, by the dynamism of His gracious gifts. Therefore, to say "yes" in faith and hope is already a willingness to act accordingly. Faith never attains fullness; it is a hopeful beginning, a constant setting out, a constantly renewed readiness to receive the Word and to act upon it. Faith thus bears the future in itself. For the believer, the future has already begun. Faith is filled with the divine promise, with the dynamic presence of salvation history that never allows us to settle down. Faith points to a clear direction, to the open horizon thus giving to the past and to the here-and-now its true fecundity.

Chapter 6

THE DYNAMISM OF HOPE:
FAITH ACTIVE IN LOVE

Hope is the dynamic force of growing faith and love. Again, we do not look upon hope or faith or love as being separate one from the other; they are alive and true to the extent that they reach a synthesis. Faith is God's gift to man whereby He reaches man's innermost being revealing Himself in love towards all men and towards the whole of creation. Through the believer, He expects to find a response of gratitude and true love. It is through God's grace in faith that man opens himself to God's own self-revealing love, thus responding to God's design to be a sharer, a concelebrant of His own love.

Faith entails a sincere openness to divine truth, to all of God's salvific revelation. The Bible is not without striking imperfections and errors in biology and astronomy because God never intended to reveal these things by miracle. The natural and physical sciences have to be learned painstakingly, but it is the Creator who gives us the power, the energy, the intelligence to discover the wonders of His creation. However, this unfolding knowledge does not constitute revelation of the salvific plan to which faith adheres. The Bible and the whole of God's revelation is without error in directing man on the path of salvation in an ever greater understanding of God's love. Even now God wants man to share as much as possible in His love, in His loving design as he makes this pilgrimage towards a perfect sharing in the beatific vision.

Will man ever realize God's salvific plan? If man does what God has indicated to him, he will realize more fully that all comes from God; he will constantly gain more light and grow in love. Where faith is severed from love, it is dead. Here we see the dangers, the pitfalls of a theology and of a catechesis that was defining faith mainly as an intellectual assent to a set of dogmas and formulas with little fruit-bearing in love. Without the dynamism of love and hope, faith is dead. To speak of faith without love and hope is comparable to defining man without life, as a corpse, a dead body already in a state of putrefaction. Who would dare say: this is man? By a miracle God can raise to life a faith that is only intellectual, that toys with formulas only, but it is no less of a miracle than the resurrection of a dead body.

Faith is really defined by a response in love, an initial response and a growing response to God revealing Himself, His love and His design to man so as to lead him on towards the final and full concelebration of His love. Therefore, it implies a faith that is alive, marked by hope and growth, openness and love. It is an initial response in love to bear fruit in love, united to God's love for man and creation. However, man's response is truthful to the extent that he remains constantly open and ready to grow in hope for final fulfilment.

In the theology of the Counter-Reformation, there was a reaction against the one-sided Protestant definition of faith where one held the assurance that God would be "my" Saviour, that one had found a merciful Saviour for oneself. The *fides fiducialis* reducing faith to one's own personal salvation was a vague and very individualistic sentiment. Catholic theology reacted by its increased concern to explain faith as a "yes" to an objective truth, as something capable of guaranteeing a community of faith. Since the Apostolic era, Christians have shared a common creed, and this aspect has to be kept; however, it is very important that we do so truly as a pilgrim Church. We share in the truth which brings salvation only when faith unites us in the readiness to act on the word, to entrust ouselves to the Lord of history in a common effort to decipher the signs of the times.

It behoves us to rid ourselves of that narrow definition of faith as intellectual assent only; it is imperative that we emphasize its hope structure and the dynamic revelation of God's loving call for a response in love and a readiness to share His love with all men. Faith, hope and love constitute the one great reality that makes man responsive to the ongoing manifestation of God's salvific plan. A life in faith, hope and love is that great reality between the first and the second coming of Christ by which God prepares us for the final event in history.

Without the dynamism towards ever greater love and ever greater hope, and without hope urging to a better knowledge of God and of man, faith is a stinking corpse. St. James says it even more drastically: "You have faith enough to believe that there is one God. Excellent! The devils have faith like that, and it makes them tremble" (James 2:19). That kind of intellectual faith divorced from the dynamism of hope and love is hell; in a barren "faith", one is condemned to sterility. However, in all humility, we must realize that the faith of the pilgrim community of faith is never sufficiently filled with love. Therefore, faith needs the hope structure, that constant yearning to know and to love God better, to respond in greater docility to His invitation, to His calling, to the manifestation of His loving design so as to serve Him better.

The foundation of our faith as well as that of our hope lies in the creative and redemptive presence of the love of God. God lovingly reveals Himself in the Covenant and restores His people through repentance, forgiveness and reconciliation to a deeper understanding of the covenant and a more faithful witness to the world. Growth in faith means a constant openness to the love of God as God reveals Himself in the context of history and in the concrete situations of daily life. I think that this vision of faith which is biblical and which was strongly emphasized in the Council by the majority of the Council Fathers and in the official conciliar documents could well preserve us from a noxious security complex. We can entrust ourselves to God totally and find a sincere obedience of faith in responsibility for the world even if we doubt some doctrines that have little or no significance for our relationship to God and brotherhood in Christ.

How many things about us are uncertain; there are so many things we would like to know better. But I dare to ask: is there not a greater assurance for us today in our vision of faith and hope and love? I think there is more certainty in the essentials today because we have come to a better understanding of the event of faith as a calling for a total commitment to God and to His plan; in this commitment we will not be shaken if, for example, there emerge different definitions of original sin or different theories of natural law provided the focal point becomes more alive in us. Even today's uncertainties which make us suffer can be signs of hope when we entrust ourselves to an ever loving God in keener awareness that God always remains infinitely greater than our concepts. When certainties in secondary things which are of no avail to our salvific life have fallen, for many the essential truths constitute a stronger pressure to entrust themselves to God in their constant search of how to respond to Him in the totality of life. Faith then acquires greater depth and attains greater firmness and fecundity.

Hope is faith and love in this in-between time. In faith we have joyously and gratefully received the One who is the Truth, the Way, the Life, and we are living in grateful response by entrusting ourselves; thus we are on pilgrimage with Him in the community of faith and hope ready to greet Him when He comes in the current events and waiting joyously for His final coming. The love we have already experienced in faith, the way God has already manifested His love draws our attention and our expectation towards that love yet unseen but promised by the very love already received. This vision of hope and faith and love also gives a certain perspective to Christian morality.

The Creed when seen in an existential way, points to our constant commitment to the glory of God in loving solidarity. *We* believe in one God, one Creator, one Father; therefore, we consider ourselves and all the gifts we have received, all our capacities and all our material gifts to have been granted in view of all of God's family. We then believe that we can rejoice in our own unique name, in our own capacities and in all that we have, only to the extent that we commit ourselves to all, to our neighbour, to the community. We believe in one Lord Jesus Christ who came not to please Himself, but to be a servant for all men. Therefore, we believe that there is no salvation for us in Christ unless we too commit ourselves with Him for the whole world, for a saving community. We can be rescued from the dark powers of evil, from the deleterious solidarity of egotists only if we too, like Christ, make ourselves servants of salvation in brotherly solidarity. He is born of the Virgin Mary, the humble maiden who pleases God for her humility, her willingness to serve and her constant Magnificat that His Church might follow her. We believe that Christ has borne the burden of all, has taken upon Himself the heavy load of the past in order to transform it and give it a new meaning. So we too believe that even the evil in our world can be transformed by us into a saving power if we bear the burdens of one another in the same spirit as Christ Jesus.

We believe that Christ gave His body to be the bread for the life of the world. In that event, the Father manifested Him as the Lord; the Father gave witness to Him by raising Him from the dead. We believe, then, that we will find our true selves, our real fulfilment by giving ourselves to our neighbour, to the community, for the life of the world. We believe in the one Holy Spirit, the Giver of all good gifts; therefore, all our hope is in solidarity if, in redeemed love, we use all the gifts, all the God-given charisms for the building up of the one Body in Christ. We believe in one holy Catholic Church; therefore, in receiving the body of Christ we recommit ourselves again and again to a constant conversion so as to become more fully the body of Christ and to strive untiringly towards Christian unity so that the Church may become more visibly a sacrament of unity for the whole of mankind. We believe in one baptism; we are baptized into solidarity and we know it will be a saving event for us if we live accordingly. Therefore, in the one hope that is held out for us, we look forward to the resurrection from the dead in the communion of the saints, for the concelebration of God's triune love.

The Creed comprises a grateful acceptance of the joyous News and a similar response; at the same time, it calls for a commitment to the salvific truth in hope and trust. It means solidarity of the community of believers in hope and a hope in solidarity based on the salvific truth in Christ who is Truth and Solidarity incarnate and thus our Hope and the hope for the whole world. Faith is an existential event through which man receives liberation, freedom in truth and in commitment to the true liberation of all. Through salvific faith, man comes out of the prison of his lonely selfishness and that of collective prejudice. Faith entails a commitment to solidarity in Christ and thus serves as an effective liberation from "original sin", from solidarity in selfishness.

Thus can we see that faith in Christ is totally different from that kind of "religion" that indulges in speculations about the number of heavenly choirs, about the principle of individuation of the angels or whether the *hymen virginale* of Mary was preserved in its physical integrity when she gave life to Jesus, and so on. Faith is not an alienation into an other-worldly hope conceived as a kind of romantic I-Thou oasis alone with "sweet Jesus" and no longer disturbed by the noise and clamour of our brothers and sisters. Truly, Christian faith and hope looking forward to life after death and the world to come is the strongest motive for a common recommitment to God's world, to the solidarity of mankind here and now. A faithful response to the truth which brings salvation uses fully the present opportunities to the honour of the One Creator and Redeemer and to the good of all His children.

Faith leads to a deeper understanding of the yearning of the created universe for freedom. Since salvation is all-embracing, the believer knows that he cannot escape the dark powers of original sin, that is, selfishness, collective injustice and prejudice, power structures and violence unless he is inserted in the one hope that comes from Christ. For Christ's sake, he is compelled to unite himself with all men of good will for the building up of a better world. This commitment to God's world in faith and hope has to be the distinctive witness of the Church as a whole, of the community of faith and love. For then only can the Church effectively be a sign of hope, a sacrament of unity for the whole of mankind, as *Lumen Gentium* says in its very first article. It is through that solidarity, that saving event, that commitment, that response to the rallying call, that we escape from the deleterious solidarity and become the great sign of hope for humanity.

The pilgrim Church faithful to the Bible and to her total tradition links together all that God has done with new events. In her faith, she sees tradition as a current of life calling for growth, for constant searching and meditation. God is still working as Christ so magnificently said to the priests and the Pharisees, the rear-guard of the Church of Israel: "My Father has never yet ceased to work, and I am working too" (John 5:17). God is in His repose, in His sabbath. He is always the same, but this does not preclude His constantly revealing Himself throughout history in new manifestations.

The hope structure of faith orients the Church's moral teaching towards a dynamic understanding of the Sermon on the Mount, more specifically towards the sevenfold "But I tell you . . ."; all point to the goal commandment to "be all goodness just as your heavenly Father is all goodness", to "love your enemies as God the Father who sends His rain and sunshine for the just and the unjust". Love expressed in great gratitude, generosity, creativity and openness, is also related to the directive of "God's own will be done on earth as it is in heaven".

The law of faith is a call to growth. Vigilance and hope help man see the next step whereas faith urges him constantly to set out, never satisfied with himself, but to set out according to the gift bestowed by Christ upon him (Eph 4:7), according to the present opportunities. So God's design is one of love for the transformation of the world through history according to the love He has manifested in Christ. He pours forth the Holy Spirit that His plan of salvation be carried on until all things are fulfilled.

Chapter 7

THE SACRAMENTALITY OF HOPE

Since God's original design for man became visible in Christ and all things are made through Him and for Him, they become visible and effective signs of hope for the believer. Therefore, we can and we should speak of the sacramental character of hope in a very broad sense. The outstanding Orthodox professor of St. Vladimir Seminary, Schmeemann, wrote a book on the sacramentality of creation [1]; this is biblical and in our best tradition. The whole of creation is a sacrament, a perceptible sign of God's presence and fidelity because it is turned towards Christ who is the fully visible sign of God's presence.

Throughout the billions of years of evolution since the creation of the universe, God's constant attention directs everything towards hominization and finally towards the point Omega, Christ Jesus, the great sign of His love. The whole evolutionary process evinces God's gracious presence steering everything towards the fullness of time, the complete divulgence of His salvific plan. By creating man and woman to His likeness, He fashions them in view of the full image of Himself which He will manifest in Christ.

Evidently, we have to move away from a mere churchly vision of sacraments for it would conceal God's word and work.

---

[1] A. Schmeemann, *Sacrament and Orthodoxy* (New York: Herder and Herder, 1965).

61

God also communicates hope in the secular world, indeed, in the whole of creation. Since He is present everywhere, He expresses His design in all His works in view of the final revelation of His Word who is to become flesh. When Christ comes, He speaks Him, He who is the great Sacrament and through Him, God expresses Himself in many sacraments, *i.e.* in all events, in all His words and deeds which make manifest the hope that the Father gives us in Him. It is by healing the sick, by feeding the hungry, by receiving the outcast, by giving sight to the blind, by siding with the victims of discriminaton that He gives us sacraments, visible signs for the greater message of eternal life. What Christ does and says is a full "word", a sign of hope for the whole person and not just for the soul. It becomes a salvific sign to hope for a healthier, more humane and just world within the greater hope for eternal life.

Throughout His life, Christ gave many signs of hope and some of them were shocking signs. Hope of this kind was unknown to the priestly class. When Christ entered into that humble dialogue with the woman of Samaria asking for water to drink and promising her a yet better water, "an inner spring always welling up to eternal life" (Jn 4:14), He made use of common everyday things: water, the well of Jacob and objects related to the quenching of thirst. Thus they became signs of that better water for which man thirsts, namely, everlasting life. He touched her own misery: the man with whom she was living was not her husband; she had had five and yet, for this woman there was hope: "I can see you are a prophet" (Jn 4:19). She could say publicly and without bitterness: "Come see the man who has told me everything I ever did. Could this be the Messiah?" (Jn 4:29). In this unusual encounter, there is no frustration; there is forgiveness and hope.

A woman who was known as a sinner in the city, probably Mary Magdalen, becomes one of the great signs of hope through Jesus Christ. The Pharisees despised her; "If this fellow were a real prophet he would know who this woman is that touches him and what sort of woman she is, a sinner" (Luke 7:39). Yet, the Lord gives her great encouragement by assuring her that she will love with that pure and grateful love which corresponds to the fullness of the mercy she receives. Not only is she a sign of hope but also the great apostle of hope on Easter morning. She who had been known as a public sinner has the privilege of bringing the message of the resurrection even to Peter and John.

Again, Christ is the great sign of hope for the woman caught in adultery. According to the Code of Hammurabi written about 1900 BC, only the woman caught in adultery was to be stoned; the man went free. In the code of Moses, both adulterous parties had to be punished but this arrogant Pharisee group brought only the woman to punishment. For her, there was no mercy; she had to be stoned. In a salvific gesture, Christ writes in the sand the sins of those righteous men and invites them: "The one among you who is without sin shall throw the first stone at her" (Jn 7:7). His mercy is saving judgment, an invitation to mercy and to conversion: "No one has condemned you?" — "No one, sir" she said. Jesus replied: "No more do I. Go in peace, but do not sin again" (Jn 7:11).

All of Christ's encounters were pledges of hope. Christ, our Hope, is the great and unique Sacrament of hope. All the other sacraments, all other events and signs receive their meaning in Him, in view of Him, the One who was, is and will come. He is the One who is constantly coming; for He is with His pilgrim Church and through her, He turns our hope to His final coming and to the here-and-now. He is coming for the world in evolution, a world in the grips of tension, a world called to judgment but finally to hope. When Christ does return, when He will hand everything and Himself over to the Father, He will no longer be a sacrament of hope. He will then be the fulfilment for all who have put their hope in Him. Meanwhile, He is the One who has come, who is coming and who will come; He is a sacrament of hope for those who are looking for His coming.

Through Christ, the pilgrim Church is a sacrament of hope and a great sacrament, but she is not automatically so in all her parts and members. She is a sacrament of hope to the extent that she accepts her role as a Church on the march, that she is ready to change and ready for that salvific discontinuity that restores her credibility as a sign of hope. She is a sign of hope if she confesses her sins and does so all over the world: "Forgive us our trespasses as we forgive those who trespass against us".

The Church is a sacrament of hope in so far as she is the mother of mercy. Where the Church in her teachings, in the utterances of her theologians and bishops assumes a rigoristic stance, she is no longer a sacrament of hope but becomes a sacrament of pessimism and despair. Jansenism did not proclaim hope; it radiated the frustration of a rigoristic, merciless church, a church for the so-called holy ones who were self-righteous but not saintly. God, the holy One, is merciful. The Church is a great sign of mercy in the sacramental sense of Mary who stands under the cross. She is a sacrament of hope to the extent that she is understanding, and realizes that even for herself, hope is an undeserved gift. She cannot proclaim her own triumphs; she proclaims the mercy of God when she models herself on the image, the prototype, the handmaid Mary, following Christ, the merciful and humble servant Messiah. Then only can she be an effective and credible sign of hope.

So the Church is one of sinners and for sinners who are striving towards holiness in mercy and in gratitude. It is only through her faith in God's gracious mercy for all men that she can have hope. How could she possibly hope in God, trust in God if she is merciless towards certain categories of men? If those who have been graced with five talents, who have a deep knowledge of God and His mercy, should be hard and merciless to others who have barely received one talent, how can they truly trust in God? How can they be a sign of hope?

The Church is a sacrament, a visible and credible sign of hope when, like Abraham leaving behind his culture and his family, she looks forward trustfully, or when, like Moses and his people who left behind the security and slavery of Egypt, she sets out into an uncertain future. Similarly did Lot leave behind him the city to be destroyed, setting out for an unknown future. In some of her members, however, the Church calls upon herself the Lord's warning: "Remember the wife of Lot" (Luke 17:32). Those who are constantly weeping and looking back to the 'good old days' are likely to become petrified monuments of pessimism. They cling to traditions which no longer express the presence of a living God and His concern for today's people; their traditions become museum items and a graveyard without hope. Hope cannot be displayed in museums; for hope is life.

The Church is a sacrament of hope as the pilgrim Church setting out into the future, leaving behind all the false and all too human securities to entrust herself fully to God, the Lord and Redeemer of history. The Church is a sacrament of hope if she courageously undergoes a thorough and painstaking soul-searching to eliminate whatever is an encumbrance on her pilgrim journey. In a Constantinian era, some of the Church's institutions were not only understandable but useful; were she to cling to these outdated structures today, the Church would only be a sign of frustration and despair. What still serves, what can still help from tradition has to be preserved. God's own word is always life and spirit, but it has to be translated into a new context.

Where Church structures cause only frustration because of an institutionalized suspicion manifested by too many controls, there is an apparent lack of trust in God. On the other hand, where people refuse any kind of human authority or guidelines, they trust more in themselves than in God. We need a healthy distrust with regard to our own weaknesses; it is a part of our trust in God, but the latter must always be greater than our distrust of human weakness. Whenever the order is reversed, we have demonology. It is a question of proportions; God is infinitely greater than all weaknesses and all powers of darkness.

A Church in the process of reform, that is becoming more aware of her imperfections, that is yearning for a more thorough-going renewal, is one that inspires hope in spite of the fact that she may yet be wanting in many respects. This is the situation of the Church of today; she has a greater awareness of her imperfections and of her need for reform. Her keener vision is God's grace and it is a sign of hope.

When the Church is in need of reform but becomes complacent, apologetic, defensive, she then becomes a counter-sacrament; take for example, the senseless and useless series of titles or the trains of the cardinals, which are now much shorter

E

though their robes are still very expensive. Last year when I was in Sicily attending the Congress of Marriage Counsellors, there happened to be an exhibit of rare animals just ouside our meeting hall. I was intrigued by a strange-looking animal whose tail was much longer than the body and I asked one of the priests: "What's the name of that animal?" Surprised, he asked in turn: "Don't you know? That's a cardinal!" We must cultivate a sense of humour as regards our weaknesses; it is a sign that there is still hope in us. We should acknowledge in gratitude towards God that many cardinals and bishops now foster a style of apostolic simplicity. They stand poles apart from the Renaissance Cardinals. Many are seeking an even more radical reform.

An outdated Canon Law is not a sign of hope. However, in spite of its obsoleteness, there is a sign of hope if people in the Church serve the Lord, not allowing themselves to transgress God's very law of love in favour of outmoded canons. If there is an effort in the Church to revise it, to adjust it in view of the needs of man and in the light of the present opportunities, then there is hope.

There are still power blocks and there are Critic Clubs, people who reinforce bitterness among themselves, who radiate so much frustration that they are strengthened in it; they truly personalize pessimism. This, however, is not the whole Church; we are blinded by an army of pessimists if we see only these flaws. We honour God if we look more to the joyous celebrations, to the courageous initiatives, to those who spread joy and peace, to the people who enjoy a good sense of humour.

There is a Church of the saints, of the humble ones, of the open-minded people, of the learners, of those who do penance, of those who forgive as God has forgiven them — and they are the Church, a visible sign of God's mercy. Before being angered and frightened by the unpleasant appearance of pessimists, we have to search for and find God's presence; He does not leave man without hope. A Church in need of freedom is a stumbling block if she is not ready to change but a Church in such a tremendous process of reform and renewal as ours is in a normal pilgrim situation and she is in this effort, in this humble avowal of her need for reform, a sacrament of hope. Those who want to anticipate the heavenly Jerusalem, who do not want to be a part of the pilgrim church, of the confessing church, of the church saying: "Forgive us our trespasses", will be scandalized by this Church.

A believer should always be both happy and unhappy about his Church, but happiness should be the predominant feeling. He praises God for keeping alive and bringing a new life to His Church. She is hopefully on the way of reform; for that we must be grateful while remaining fully aware of our own need for redemption and renewal, of the need of the whole Church to be more consciously a pilgrim Church, one which is imperfect yet accepts the call to holiness with growing vigilance for present opportunities. The Church in her very imperfection, which will always be a part of her life in time, is a prognostic sign as indicated by the Church Fathers, *i.e.* a sign drawing our hopes to the life beyond history while strengthening our energies while en route to fullness of life.

There is hope in history in the saints, the converted people, the humble ones, those who remain alert in a life of prayer and service to the poor; yet, the totality does not allow us to confuse the earthly with the heavenly Jerusalem. We are yearning for the heavenly Jerusalem. We must then learn humility and an understanding of Christian life as a constant conversion and reform.

In Christian hope, there is always a prophetic element, a protest against what falls short of God's graciousness, what does not respond to the call for a more painstaking examination of conscience, to a greater readiness for conversion. In this prophetic dissent, the live protest of those who are in full solidarity with the Church, there is hope. In the non-violent, prophetic protest there is no resignation. Those who carry on this kind of protest will never be heard saying that there are hopeless people, hopeless situations because there will always be a worthy effort on their part.

While criticism without hope and without initiative for change spells frustration and bitterness, there can be a criticism inspired by love and accompanied by deeds opening onto new horizons;

this is a sign of hope. It gives credit and it deserves it. There is a futile criticism which wastes time lamenting over bad structures, outdated laws and backlashes, where the critics remain unconcerned about their own conversion and their possible contribution to a better atmosphere in the Church. Only those parts of the Church that are equally concerned with reform of structures and their personal conversion render honour to God and inspire hope. They are mindful of the need for a better world, for improved surroundings and for a more holy people; in the fullest sense, they constitute a sign or a sacrament of hope.

If the Church wants to be ever more fully a sacrament of hope, she has to overcome all the security complexes. Of course, since there are different people there must, for instance, be different religious congregations; we need some conservative groups that can provide a home for people with a greater need for security. However, the whole Church should not be a home for insecure people. If we need mental asylums for sick people, we cannot expect the whole Church to become a mental asylum. There must be room for different characters, varied temperaments, but as a whole, the Church must not be sick with that insecurity that wants to guarantee unity through a uniform Canon Law or an inflexible liturgy that does not allow any spontaneity. In spite of the fact that Latin has gone, we have not yet totally overcome the mentality which was seeking unity by imposing one language and forms of Latin thought on Christians of all cultures.

Newsmen have approached me recently and asked what kind of changes in Church structures I would make if I had my way; they pointedly asked: would you do away with the Monsignori and the Cardinalate? I replied firmly in the negative to which they seemed surprised; however, I qualified my answer by saying that I would see to it that people interested in these titles knew exactly what they meant. I would provide one canon that would read thus: "Every priest who indulges in vanity has a right to be named Monsignor and to call himself 'the Very Right and Reverend Monsignor'. If he can prove his ineptitude for anything else, he is entitled to become a super-Monsignor; however, he would have to pay half of his income to the missions for such a privilege. He would be allowed to wear all colours of vestments but never in holy places; he would have to promise not to get angry at people who are amused by his vanity." For the cardinals, I would do something similar. The conditions would be that they must be at least 80 to be nominated; it would have to be proved that they are incapable of any new initiative, etc. The conditions could be stated in such a way that no great Churchman would ever aspire to such positions and titles. Of course, the election of the successor of Saint Peter would not be the business of men eighty years old or more. In my opinion, the institution of Monsignori with its various levels and that of the Cardinalate are signs of an outdated era. However, new things are arising so that we can smile at some remnants of the triumphalistic age of the Church.

We have a problem in the Church and we must face it realistically; there must be room for the old people, some place of honour where they can retire. For example, in Rome we have the Chapters of the Canons of St. Mary Major and of St. John Lateran; they are good institutions in the sense that some people would no longer be capable of an active post. Here at least, they can be promoted and will no longer interfere with progress. It is a nod to human weakness; everyone knows that these people cannot function adequately in responsible positions and would not be happy without honours, titles and ostentatious colours. Again, let us cultivate a sense of humour for human weakness.

However, should such structures be presented as belonging to the very core of the Church, should they receive serious attention as in wide publicity, then they will be a source of frustration. Knowing that we are in a period of transition can help us focus on positive signs with the strength of trust in God, with that sense of humour which will allow us to see all of today's new signs of hope. We can then deal more realistically with problems because there are greater signs of hope: God's presence in His Church, His promise never to let it be without hope.

The Church is a sacrament of hope, but we must never forget that Christ alone is our Hope, the true Sacrament of hope. All the other realities are visible and effective signs only to the extent that they turn all our attention and trust to Christ.

A great deal of frustration arises precisely when one puts all one's trust in the institutional aspect of the Church. One loses sight of the prophetic aspect and becomes disillusioned and disappointed. A right understanding of the Church shows the following three qualities: (1) it turns all our hope to God in Christ Jesus; (2) it does not underestimate the prophetic-charismatic element in the Church and (3) it pays attention to all that God does in the world. If often we are so deeply disappointed in men or in the Church it is because we have put all our hope in them or we are victims of shortsightedness. The sacramentality of the Church and of all created things can only have meaning if it helps to a greater trust in God, and in God alone. The officeholder in the Church is entitled to trust and confidence but it can never be an absolute trust.

The feelings of despair and bitterness stemming from institutional weaknesses and faults of men in the "system" are often due to a narrow concept of the Church. In the Church there are many ministries and charisms. The officeholders may occasionally give a wrong impression by their seeming identification with the Church as institution or with authority. If the Church of the Old and of the New Testament becomes a sign of hope, it is particularly through the prophetic men and women whom God sends us in His mercy. When we try to envisage the unity of all the different ministries, we realize that the healthy conflicts arising temporarily are necessary growing pains much like the pangs of childbirth.

Just as the officeholders in the Church must not think of themselves as "the Church", similarly must the Church as a whole never give the impression that she monopolizes the action of God in the world. She is more truly a sign of hope if she opens her eyes to all the good which God works throughout history in men the world over.

The Synod of Bishops is a tremendous sign of hope. That Pope Paul, after serious discussion and serious challenges, has agreed to have the world episcopate select the permanent advisors to the Secretariate of the Synod, and that the bishops have an active voice with regard to setting the great themes of the meetings scheduled every other year — these are great signs of hope, signs that new structures are replacing the old ones.

Chapter 8

THE SACRAMENTS OF CHRISTIAN HOPE

The broader concept of sacramentality in the Church and the world inevitably leads us to the seven sacraments of the Church which are often referred to as "sacraments of faith" or "sacraments of hope". The vision of sacramentality that extends to all signs of God's presence, that awaken trust and hope in Him and gratitude for His gifts, and make men instruments of peace and hope, helps us to a better appreciation of the seven sacraments. Therefore, in introducing these signs of hope, I insist on the proper perspective.

The idea is classically expressed by St. Augustine who had to respond to the question: How can the sacraments be signs of salvation when we keep them from the heathen? He turns the attention of all to the Cross of the Redeemer where we find the mystery of the hidden God effectively revealing His infinite love. "With deep roots and on firm foundation, may you be strong to grasp, with all God's people, what is the breadth, length, height and depth of the love of Christ. Perhaps this is the Cross of our Lord. There is the breadth of the arms stretched out to all; there is the depth which gives firmness to the whole Cross where all the hope of our life stands firmly rooted. Then the breadth will not be lacking in our good deeds where there is the length of perseverance to the end. The good deeds have their height when the heart dwells above with Christ, so that in their full length and breadth of goodness all the good deeds

73

arise from the hope of the heavenly reward. The height means that we do not look for an earthly remuneration so that it will not be said of us 'they already have their reward' (Mt 6:2). The depth, as already stated, is that hidden part of the Cross rooted in the earth which gives it a support and firmness for all to see the Cross. But what is that hidden part, I mean, what is hidden in the Church? I respond: the sacrament of Baptism and the sacrament of the Eucharist. But while the sacraments remain hidden to the heathen, they can see your good deeds. What is visible arises from that depth which they cannot perceive much like the hidden part of the Cross that rises and is visible." [1]

Saint Augustine thus envisages the celebration and reception of the sacraments in their essential dynamism towards life. The faithful who live according to the gift and mission coming through the sacraments become the visible signs of hope and of salvation for those who do not know the sacraments.

The sacraments prove to be sacraments of hope for us if, through them, we come to know Christ better and reveal Him through our witness. In other words, we truly accept the grace and mission of the sacraments if, in turn, we become "sacraments", visible and efficacious signs of hope for the world around us.

In order to enter more fully into the biblical perspective and the great vision of the earlier centuries, we must strive to free ourselves of an all too technical concept of the sacraments; they must not be looked upon as a "sacramental system" with inflexible rules. It is helpful to recall that the Church herself could be a sacrament and could celebrate the sacraments for eleven centuries without ever attempting to count their number. It was Peter Lombard in the twelfth century who first stated that the Church had seven and only seven sacraments. This theologian remained, for centuries, very influential even beyond his merits owing to the fact that the work of Thomas Aquinas had been placed on the Index of Forbidden Books by the arch-

---

[1] Augustine, *En. in Psalmum CIII*, PL 37, 348.

bishop of Paris and remained practically unavailable until the sixteenth century.

It must be said that Peter Lombard used good criteria for establishing the number seven: a sacrament had to be a salvific sign instituted by Christ for all times and for all His disciples for the good of the whole Church. Before him, however, almost all treatises on the sacraments included washing of the feet because Christ had washed the feet of His Apostles; it was also a common practice. As a liturgical rite, however, it was considered a sacrament only when one thereby committed himself to Christ, the Servant. The ritual performance would be true to one's whole life, would be a sacrament only if one then rendered the most humble service to whoever needed it. Wherever, through God's gracious presence, His kindness and mercy shine through to win man's heart, there is a sacrament in the broader sense of the term.

From the beginning, the sacraments were celebrated in the Church in faith, gratitude and hope. Validity had not yet become technically problematic, but no sacrament would have made sense to Christians if it had not been a sign of hope inspiring to even greater hope and trust. One of the reasons for this hope lies in the very fact that the sacraments as instituted by Christ held definite promises. When celebrating them in accord with the intent of Christ, we receive an ever new assurance of His goodness, mercy and fidelity; we become transformed into ever more visible signs of hope for the world around us. The celebration and reception of the sacraments in the community of hope transfigures the participants into signs of solidarity in hope and hope in salvific solidarity. That is why the sacraments can be called a privileged school of hope.

The sacraments are manifestations of God's graciousness, of His attractive countenance turning to man. Each sacrament then becomes an interpersonal encounter between man and God. There is a strong emphasis on God's initiative, His undeserved goodness, kindness and mercy in establishing this relationship. In so far as Christians accept the sacraments as God's benevolent initiative and appreciate them as God's gifts, to that extent are

75

they outstanding signs of hope. As sanctifying events, they constitute a new perspective for and add new dimensions to the most basic human experiences. In presenting the sacraments and explaining their celebration as a great sign of hope, it is most important that the liturgical ceremony clearly indicate their dynamism in one's personal life.

While maintaining this frame of reference, we can now consider the seven sacraments in turn. We look upon them as privileged signs of hope and as a privileged school of hope and of all the other eschatological virtues which will be treated later.

As an efficacious sign of hope in solidarity, *baptism*'s dimension derives from Christ's own baptism. In the Gospel of St. Luke, we read that Christ was baptized by St. John the Baptist during a general baptism. At that moment, the heavens opened, the Spirit came visibly upon Him and the voice of the Father was heard saying: "Thou art my Son, my Beloved; on thee my favour rests" (Lk 3:22). Christ presented Himself in the crowd of tax-gatherers ready to make restitution, among soldiers who had been blackmailing others, prostitutes and similar unclean people who knew they were poor but who hoped for redemption. The Pharisees were not there. During the general baptism of people very much aware of their need for forgiveness, Christ presented Himself to make known that He was bearing their burdens, thus revealing the meaning of His cross as the great baptism. In the same Gospel of St. Luke, Christ refers to His death on the cross: "I have a baptism to undergo, and how hampered I am until the ordeal is over" (Lk 12:50). We can say that Christ was baptized in His own blood for all men, "to set fire to the earth" (Lk 12:49), preparing the new earth and the new heaven where love and unity will reign.

Baptism inserts us in the hope-inspiring reality that Christ bears our burden, that by His life-blood He calls us to be His brothers and sisters. He introduces us to that saving solidarity which is manifested in the ritual baptism of the Jordan and in the life-blood baptism, *i.e.*, in the liturgy and in life and death. So it is an insertion into the community of salvation with Christ who freed us from the deleterious solidarity in sinfulness. As members of the community of faith, we are sharers in the gladdening news. As members in the community of hope, we are committed to the building of a better milieu, of one promoting a more humane and faithful life. We are effectively inserted into the community of hope when we become initiators of hope, having first received the undeserved sign of hope. Then we should become ever greater signs of hope in the course of our lifetime. That baptism is a sign of hope should be visible especially in the way we celebrate the great event; all in attendance should come to realize that by being baptized into the saving solidarity in Christ, into the body of Christ, we are directed towards the Eucharist, the great sign of unity, and towards a life in accord with these two great signs of hope.

The *Eucharist* is the central experience of faith, of the waiting in joyful expectation for the coming of our Saviour Jesus Christ. Since it is a "sacrament", it should become visible, moving both heart and mind by the way in which it is celebrated. Therefore, we may ask: what kind of sacrament is a Eucharistic celebration where no joy and hope shine forth, where no encouragement is received? The Eucharist is the great sign of the baptism of Christ who extends His arms for all, giving hope to all; it is the awaiting of the blessed coming in the community of the hopeful, the joyful expectancy of the pilgrim Church.

It follows that a priest capable of concelebrating Mass with his confrères but who insists on celebrating "the visible sign of unity" in splendid isolation becomes a countersign. I am not referring to priests who are incarcerated and cannot concelebrate, or others who are psychologically incapacitated. The offender is he who does not like the community of others and who, therefore, in his self-imposed isolation, celebrates original sin. He does not meet Christ as a sign of hope and solidarity for the community and in the community. His celebration is not the sacrament that manifests to others or brings to his personal life any promise of hope. Concelebration, however, makes sense only if the gracious command of brotherhood and solidarity is perceived and reconfirmed. We are called to concelebrate God's love with all God's people and to yearn for the oneness of the priestly people of God and the ministerial priesthood.

A loveless celebration fails to be truly and fully a sacrament, a visible sign of hope. It would be helpful if occasionally we were to ask ourselves: what does Christ want me to do as a pilgrim coming to Him? The Eucharist can alert us to His coming in daily events while we await His final coming.

The Eucharist has to score all the dimensions of our faith by bringing to the fore our thanksgiving for the great signs of hope in the past: the creation, the incarnation, Christ's death and ascension, the mission of the Holy Spirit. Our personal experiences have to be brought to the Eucharist so that all together, with all that we share, we look forward in a community of faith and of hope to the final coming of the Lord.

Confirmation is the sacrament of growth towards maturity in docility to the Spirit. It is a sign of hope through which Christ calls us insistently to the blessed freedom of the sons and daughters of God. It signifies the fullness of times when we allow ourselves to be led by the Spirit, the giver of all good gifts. Thus we regain a mature perspective on Christian life, open ourselves to the needs of others, being vigilant always for present opportunities. The Spirit frees us from selfish concern to make us instruments of peace and justice, signs of hope for many. It assimilates us to Christ "who did not consider Himself". Consecrated by His Spirit, "each of us must consider his neighbour and think what is for his good and will build up the common life" (Rom 15:2).

When adults come to faith, the sacrament of confirmation constitutes a part of the total celebration of initiation into the community of faith and hope. It is a commitment to solidarity through consecration by the Spirit in whom Christ has consecrated Himself for His brethren. In the case of infant baptism, it seems advisable to receive confirmation at the age of initiation into the adult world and public life. The choice of one's own state of life and profession should be cast in the light of this sacrament of hope in mature solidarity.

Most of the ancient cultures had a solemn moment of initiation for the young people. It was most appropriate for the sacrament of confirmation to be related to this decisive social and personal event. Particularly in African cultures, the initiation rites had and to some extent still have an extraordinary relevance for the assumption of social responsibilities. In many tribes, initiation provided a very strong psychological and religious motivation for premarital chastity and other important social virtues. Unfortunately, in many parts of Africa, missionaries were hostile to the whole practice of initiation and by doing away with it, deprived the African people of all the inherited and needed psychological and social support. Instead, they should have followed the lead of the earlier Church and brought the traditional initiation into the full light of confirmation.

Confirmation fulfils the hopes and promises which were contained in the traditional initiation and it should become a sign of genuine continuity. Since initiation is an important aspect of tribal and family life, the preparation for confirmation and its celebration should integrate all the good of the past and thus pave the way for the future. Where Christian faith takes deeper roots it would not be too difficult to reshape and to revitalize the initiation rites in a sense that would promote the maturation not only of the individual but also of the community and culture.

The sacrament of *reconciliation* makes clear to man that he is the beneficiary of God's undeserved Shalom. God's peace comes to him; he receives it only if he accepts it, if he is transformed into a messenger of peace, if he is shaped by God's own forgiveness and can forgive others. One receives it best and is aware of having received it when he is a visible and effective sign of peace and reconciliation for others on all levels.

The Sacrament of Shalom or of reconciliation should be that outstanding personal experience of God's mercy in the Church and through the Church meant to be a sacrament of compassion and mercy. But when a person enters a dark box and is separated by a wall behind which growls a tiger, how can the sacrament of peace be visible? A sacramental celebration involving a depersonalized being who relies on solutions of casuistry which he applies mechanically to an unknown and unseen person cannot possibly be in accord with Christ's intent. The very meaning of visible sign obliges the Church to reform the practices and to renew the celebration of the sacrament in a way that speaks to the man of today.

Marriage becomes a sacrament, a visible sign of an experience of hope to the extent that the spouses trust each other, faithfully keep their promises and forgive one another. The juridical marriage contract by itself, if it is not followed by a covenant of love, can become more a cause of despair than a sign of hope. But marriage vows expressed after serious preparation and in all sincerity are a pledge that can inspire a deeper understanding of God's promise in the new and everlasting covenant. We must not minimize the fact that an effective sacramentality of marriage depends on the degree to which hope and trust, kindness and mutual understanding become visible.

A few years ago, I spoke on marriage validity and asked those in attendance which of two cases they would consider to be more of a sacrament. The responses varied and some were quite contradictory. The first case was a mixed marriage declared invalid because the pastor, refusing to grant the dispensation, necessitated that the marriage be celebrated in the Lutheran Church. Canonically, the marriage was invalid; however, these two persons loved each other dearly, prayed together, helped one another get closer to God and were the first messengers of the Gospel to their children. After fifty years when the marriage was being canonically validated, the priest asked: "Mr. Miller, do you accept Miss Schneider as your valid spouse?"

The second case involved a marriage which met all Canon Law regulations; the priest had spent two hours looking for impediments and had found none. The marriage was then celebrated according to proper jurisdiction. However, these two persons never cared for one another, never prayed together, never shared a word about God. On the contrary, they consistently frustrated one another. Where is the sacrament?

Of course, there is something lacking in the first case but

lacking chiefly on the part of that canonist or that priest who locked the institutional door. However, the Holy Spirit is not hampered by human mishandling. It is through God's gift and man's generous response that a marriage can work out as a sacrament.

The way the line is drawn between valid and invalid marriages is at present a distressing problem in many parts of the world but particularly in Africa whose cultures are not made for our mediterranean Canon Law. In numerous tribes, if the marriage is not blessed with children after two or three years, it is torn asunder by the clan, whether the spouses like it or not. Both families want to disprove that sterility is on their side. Often enough, both partners in a second marriage boast of as many as ten or twelve children and live happily together. If the first marriage was blessed in the Church, most of the diocesan officials consider it indissoluble in spite of the fact that the condition "if it becomes fertile" is deeply written in the whole culture and in the heart and mind of the contracting parties. Some priests tend to encourage a canonical celebration of the marriage only after children are born; in the meantime, they exclude these spouses from the sacraments because, in their eyes, these people live in plain fornication. Others bless the first marriage but give no hope to those who, after their marriage is torn asunder, live in a second stable marriage. Is not their family life with all the love, fidelity, forbearance, good education of the children a sign of hope in the perspective of salvation?

A priest in Africa told me a few years ago: "I have 23,000 Catholics and they are all religious people. If I were to observe all the rules of Canon Law, I would have to excommunicate 80% of them. However, I do not; I look to the good will. I cannot possibly go through all the details of canonical legislation; I have 2000 catechumens and only one assistant. Were I to heed all canonical processes in relation to marriage, I would be a frustrated administrator with no time to preach the Gospel."

I do not deny the right of the Church to lay down certain rules on which depend acknowledgment of marriage. However, the emphasis must not be one-sidedly on canonical validity, but rather, greater attention should be given that each marriage

F

become truly, in daily life, an effective sign of hope. This requires a more careful preparation for marriage and a constant care for the spouses' growth in marital love. During the celebration of marriage and throughout their life, the spouses should learn to link hope for everlasting life with their marriage covenant. It is God who entrusts them to each other and remains with them so that they can love one another with a redeemed and redeeming love. They are not seeking absolute and final beatitude in their marriage; therefore, they will not so easily be frustrated when their illusions collapse and they have to bear with their mutual weaknesses. Hope in God's forbearance will inspire a generous readiness for forgiveness. Marriage is a realm of hope if the spouses learn together to put all their hope in God and to view their mutual trust only as a puzzling mirror-image of their trust in God. If they love each other in spite of all their weaknesses and failures, they grow in understanding of God's undeserved and tender love.

The irrevocable commitment sanctioned by the Church and celebrated before the Church is a beginning, a sign of hope, that God will fulfil what He has begun if they pray and cooperate with His grace. It is not primarily the canonical sanctions but rather the inner power of God's grace coupled with their mutual love graced by trust in God that guarantees effectively the indissolubility of their covenant.

The Church's canonical regulation for marriage and her pastoral care are a sign of hope if she blends the call to fidelity with a demonstrable understanding, compassion and mercy. The Church cannot proclaim reconciliation to that person who has deserted his spouse leaving him/her waiting for a return, unless the culprit does his best to seek reconciliation. However, in cases where the first marriage can in no way be restored, if we find absolute good will in people living in a canonically invalid marriage which, notwithstanding, bears the marks of love, commitment and dedication, there must be a serious effort on the part of the Church to manifest herself and her sacraments as signs of hope.

In a number of cases, there is ample evidence that the first marriage never deserved the name of "sacrament" and that, even canonically, it was not valid. I cannot see why, in such cases, pastors and confessors should cooperate so fully with those officials—canonists, who demand 101% proof of the invalidity of the first marriage while, with less than 1% proof, they cast these people away from the sacraments of the Church. We will return later to this burning question that has so much to do with the right understanding of the Church and her sacraments as signs of hope for all men of good will.

In this context, I offer only one suggestion with regard to the so-called "insoluble marriage cases". I often counsel such couples thus: "Although I cannot do anything to get your marriage into the parish register, I advise you to pray together and do your best to make your present marriage a true sign of love and of hope, a community of faith. Be signs of hope and of God's own love for your children. Be faithful to one another. If your love becomes ever more redeemed and profound, you may consider this a sign that God is graciously present to you and gives you hope." My position may seem strange to some, but I believe that through God's grace, a marriage can become very much an effective sign of grace and hope although the canonists are not willing to cooperate in any way to give it the status of a sacrament.

The *ministerial priesthood* of the Church is an efficacious sign of hope to the extent that priests are assimilated to Christ who is at the same time the High Priest who gives Himself as ransom for His people and the Prophet who rejects any idle *status quo*. Christ detests ritualism, formalism and everything that stifles trust in God, the longing and striving towards greater union with God and better realization of brotherhood.

Christ is the great sign of hope particularly by His perfect synthesis of love of God with love of neighbour. He listens to the Father while attending to the needs and prayers of the people; He proclaims forgiveness of sins and eternal life while taking care of the diseased and the hungry. He is the hope of all since He did not come to be served but to serve. A priest is a visible sign of hope if, not only with words and sacramental rites but also by his life and his relationship to the people, he makes visible Christ, the great sign of hope for all. He makes visible God's gracious presence if he is not so much a "specialist in religion", in rubrics and laws as a graced, gracious servant of the economy of salvation. The present unrest relative to the understanding of the priesthood and the search for new forms and structures is a yearning for the ministerial priesthood to be more visibly a sign of hope for the men of today. All want a hope that transcends all earthly hopes but which, to some extent, incarnates the hopes of daily life as Christ's priesthood was related to the joys and hopes of men.

Celibacy for the heavenly kingdom is not a sacrament in the technical sense but it is a great sign of hope if freely chosen or accepted in faith. When without human planning divine Providence leads to celibacy, if it is lived in joyful expectation of the coming of the Saviour and in vigilance for the needs of others, one witnesses to the total vocation and hope of man in Christ.

Illness and the expectation of death are moments of temptation; many hopes seem to collapse in the gravely ill. Suffering can disturb and frustrate the mind. Through the sacrament of the *anointing of the sick,* Christ encounters the sick and his family telling them that all suffering is redeemed and plays a role in the redemption of mankind when it is united with His death and resurrection. Those who entrust themselves in their illness to Christ and who embrace death as a salvific event number among the most valuable signs and testimonies of the total hope to which Christ calls us.

There are many situations in life where God bestows on us many gracious signs. "Sacramental spirituality"[1] is not limited to these seven sacraments; however, they do open all the horizons, give the right perspective, make people aware of God's presence in life's situations. God, through the gracious persons who are truly sacraments, makes His people more aware of His presence and of His goodness.

------

[1] See my book, *A Sacramental Spirituality* (New York: Sheed and Ward, 1965).

Chapter 9

THE JOYFUL CHARACTER OF HOPE

The Christian religion is not just a system of ethics or a series of commandments; neither can it be restricted to a *commandment* of love. The religious faith of a Christian consists in life with Christ, the fulfilled promise and the final promise of fulfilment.

The impact of Karl Marx's ideology came from its promise of a better world. We are entitled to ask: why is it that Communism's thrust is now dying if not dead? Personally, I think Communism as ideology died two years ago in Prague; at least for Czechoslovakia and the greater part of Eastern Europe, it has faded away because of its failure to keep any of its major promises and its pledges for the future are untrustworthy.

In historical retrospect the short-lived influence of Communist hope can be accounted for in religious terms. When Marx began his career, for too many Christians religious doctrine consisted mainly of a catalogue of commandments. Catholics regarded minor man-made fast-and-abstinence law and the Eucharist as equally important. Meatless Fridays were enjoined with as much vigour as Sunday Mass, and the latter had become chiefly a legal ordinance. For many commitment to work for a more fraternal world was either an unknown or an irrelevant Christian notion. In short, religion had degenerated into concern about saving one's own soul and maintenance of the *status quo* in society. Such was the social and religious setting in which the poor eked out a meagre existence.

When Karl Marx proposed his ideas, wrong as they were, they offered a mighty hope, a promise of better things to come. Even the suffering of the oppressed proletariat was regarded by him as a positive factor leading to the final explosion of hatred in the form of revolution and the establishment of eventual brotherhood in a classless society. His whole theory of hope was rooted in aggression's opening doors to a future of everlasting peace.

Many other worldly messianisms are being proposed in this day and age and they will probably exert their seductive influence on people unless Christianity becomes what it should be according to the will of Christ: the greatest of all promises. "The world belongs to whoever offers it the greater hope." From beginning to end, the Christian religion is one of promise, hope and fidelity. It should be enlightening for all to see how the Christians of apostolic times looked upon Christ's life, death and the proclamation of His joyful message.

The first synthesis of apostolic catechesis is presented in the gospel of Mark; it summarizes Christ's whole life, being and preaching. "Christ began to proclaim the gladdening news coming from God. The time of favour has come, the kingdom of God is upon you; be renewed in your mind and believe in the Gospel" (Mk 1: 14-15). Be renewed in your mind by putting your trust in the gladdening news; this is the gist of the message, the full scope of a very short synthesis.

As divine Messenger living in close proximity to the people, Christ proclaims the good news and does so with authority. He has come to gladden the hearts and minds of people. "The time of favour" refers to promises made earlier; had not the prophets spoken of that time when the Messenger of peace would proclaim the gladdening news? Christ begins His mission by preaching in the synagogue at Nazareth; He reads the scroll: "The spirit of the Lord is upon me because the Lord has anointed me; he has sent me to bring good news to the humble" (Lk 4: 18). He is the fulfilment of the prophecies; the promises of the Old

Testament are now fulfilled in Him; for He has come to bring joy, peace and hope.

Whatever Christ is and does serves as a preparation for the resurrection; it is a message of joy and an overture to happiness. Christ does not indulge in a sterile moralism or bare law because the law can never bring the fullness of life. Furthermore, if the law has forfeited its real liberating power, if it becomes a dead law, this is due to our selfish self. Faith in the good tidings and trust in Christ who is the gladdening news spell the difference between Christ's teaching and mere moralism. In summary, Christ proclaims the gladdening message in His person, in His word and finally in His death and resurrection. For this the Spirit has anointed and sent Him; He in turn sends the Spirit in whom we can joyously cry out, "Abba, Father". The essence of Christian morality is then a renewal of heart and mind by putting our faith and trust in the Gospel, in the good tidings. Christ's message is one of hope but hope in the full existential meaning of entrusting ourselves to Christ, our peace and our Gospel, who is most desirous that we in turn become messengers of joy.

The Sermon on the Mount as recorded in St. Matthew served as apostolic catechesis in preparation for the sacraments of initiation, *i.e.*, baptism and confirmation, and the Eucharist. The evangelist emphasizes the fact that Christ communicates His beatitudes, His message of joy and rule of life in the presence of the crowd; it is not intended just for a few. Surrounded by His disciples, Jesus opens His mouth and delivers the following message: "How blest are those . . ." nine times repeated (Mt 5:1-7). He communicates His own joy, His own beatitude, His own love, mercy and gentleness. By His whole being and, as pointed out by the Church Fathers, by the mission of the Holy Spirit, He truly gathers all his disciples on the mount of the beatitudes. He communicates to true believers His joy and the blessedness of the Paschal Mystery. The Servant of God and of men who is also the Truth of salvation, the Way and the Life, He is bearer of joy and source of joy. His joyous message by far takes precedence over the commandments; indeed, the commandments have no meaning for those who do not recognize Him as the source of joy, peace and hope.

In Luke's Sermon on the Plain, it is reported that people came to Him from Jerusalem, Judea, Samaria and from the heathen cities because power went out from Him, an attractive and healing power (Lk 6: 17-19). He then communicated joy but with a clear understanding that those who do not accept Him as its source and who do not open themselves to His message of joy and consequently do not follow Him on this road are passing judgment on themselves. Woe to them! Without Him, there is no joy and no hope; He is the Messenger of joy, hope and peace.

Before presenting the great commandment, the all-embracing directive to "love one another as I have loved you" (Jn 15: 12), Jesus says: "All this I have spoken to you that my joy may be in you and your joy may be complete" (Jn 15: 11). Only those who open themselves to His message of joy, who treasure it up in their hearts can bear fruit for the life of the world: "If you dwell in Me and My words dwell in you, ask what you will, and you shall have it. This is My Father's glory, that you may bear fruit in plenty and so be My disciples" (Jn 15: 7-8). Only if, like Mary (Lk 2: 19), we cherish in our hearts the saving message, the gladdening word, only if it truly dwells in our hearts to be pondered over, shall we bear fruit in love. His word, which is love and joy, desires to dwell in us so that we can communicate His life and joy to the world.

The whole teaching of the Gospel, the preaching of the apostles and the letters of St. Paul make clear that we shall be sterile and our life will be barren if we close ourselves to the message of joy. Moralism can be the most hopeless business in the world if we begin by imposing a commandment instead of first communicating joy. I feel that the Super-Skunk has done a very effective job in many parts of the world with bare injunctions, prescriptions, prohibitions, do's and don'ts; his effectiveness has resulted in absolute joylessness and the noticeable sterility of much of Christian life.

In His high-priestly prayer, Jesus says: "While I am still in the world, I speak these words so that they may have joy within them in full measure" (Jn 17: 13). The purpose of His coming was to bring us His joy in fullness. If we cherish His words, His expressions of joy, the communication of His beatitude, and if we consent to follow Him who paved the way for us in the Paschal Mystery, we shall then know the full measure of His joy and will bear the fruit for which Christ prayed: unity, oneness made possible by putting to death our selfish desires. It is not possible for man to conquer his selfishness unless he trusts in Christ and believes in the gladdening news of Christ.

The Gospels clearly indicate that the earliest efforts of the apostolic communities to synthesize Christ's life and message depict Him as the Messenger of joy and the call to faith. For us, this means a joyous acceptance and treasuring up of His words, allowing them to dwell in us so that they will take on the dynamism which will eventually manifest itself in bearing the fruits of love, joy and peace for the life of the world. Christ's "command" is a word of joy, of grace, communicating His own love and joy.

At all times St. Paul appears as a messenger of joy, preaching incessantly Christ's message of joy. In spite of his many frustrating experiences and captivity, Paul writes to the Philippians: "Yes, and rejoice I will, knowing well that the issue of it all will be my deliverance, because you are praying for me and the Spirit of Jesus Christ is given me for support" (Phil 1: 19). So it is not only in spite of trials but even because of them and the sufferings uniting him to the Paschal Mystery that Paul can say "yes" and rejoice, for he knows well that the issue of all his trials will be his deliverance because "you are praying for me and the Spirit of Jesus Christ is given me for support. For, as I passionately hope, I shall have no cause to be ashamed, but shall speak so boldly that now as always the greatness of Christ will shine out clearly in my person, whether through my life or through my death" (Phil 1: 19-21). The greatness of Christ shines through in both life and death. "For to me life is Christ and death gain" (Phil 1: 22). "Only let your conduct be worthy of the Gospel of Jesus Christ" (Phil 1: 27). The word "Gospel" means the effective communication of joy and hope.

Paul's whole life becomes an encouragement and a source of hope to early Christians; he rejoices while in jail, while being flogged, while being despised because he knows that in all his trials, the Paschal Mystery is working salvation for him and through him. But for his beloved disciples and for himself personally, the condition is that their life and conduct be worthy of the gladdening news of the Gospel of Christ. Thus with Christ he can face death in hope. Christ made death the great sign of trust: "But if my life-blood is to crown that sacrifice which is the offering up of your faith, I am glad of it and I share my gladness with you all. Rejoice, you no less than I, and let us share our joy" (Phil 2:17-18). It is while in captivity and while suffering injustice that Paul preaches this message of peace and joy. Similarly, St. Ignatius of Antioch, while being "chained to seven leopards" and expecting to be thrown to the lions, sends a message of joy to Rome: he comes to sacrifice his life and they should not hinder him; for believers, there is reason to rejoice in martyrdom. Such is the strength of faith in the Paschal Mystery.

Three times Paul attempts to bring to a close and sign off his letter to the Philippians; each time, it is with "I wish you joy in the Lord." The third time, he repeats: "I wish you all joy in the Lord. I will say it again: all joy be yours" (Phil 4:4).

In the Epistle to the Galatians, when he sets down the basic rules or criteria for the discernment of genuine love from its counterfeits, he assigns the first place to love and posits joy and peace as immediate manifestations of it (Gal 5:22). Then follow those attitudes indicative of peace: patience, kindness, goodness, gentleness and self-control. These are the signs, the criteria we must observe if we want to know what applies in our times, whom we should follow and from whom we should learn. These attitudes are conspicuously absent in angry, bitter people and in institutional critics whether they be theologians, canonists, bishops, superiors or infallible young or old people.

At the end of his term in the jails of South Africa, Gandhi sent a word of peace, a message of goodness to General Gordon who had unjustly imprisoned him. While in prison, he had made a pair of sandals for him. Gandhi informed him that he would continue his nonviolent action against suppression and racial discrimination; however, he would do so convinced that on the other side there are people capable, ultimately, of accepting the message of peace. When in India he started to work out his theology of nonviolent action and to gather a group of leaders about him, he first began by opening an *ashram* or house of prayer, a worthy legacy for all of us. Only if we are united with God will He preserve peace, and will our actions promote peace in the world.

It matters very little in these times of polarization whether one calls oneself a liberal or a conservative; what truly matters is whether we join the frustrated, bitter and angry people or align ourselves with the peaceful, kind, hopeful and joyful people of God. After listening for more than an hour to a class of deacons verbalizing their dissatisfaction, I finally spoke out: "You are all just reactionaries; you have not offered one constructive comment nor uttered a peaceful word; you are only pitting yourselves against reactionaries." There is a definite danger that criticism will become bitter and frustrated; when this happens, nothing more can be learned. Of course, those who first caused the frustration should not then counter reactionary criticism with more bitter criticism. It is then time for everybody to come to his senses, to give in and pray for peace. The criterion in this case should not be so much readiness to change as the basic Christian attitude of joy and peace. It should then be possible to see the direction which change should take. So once again, we are faced with the fundamental question: where do we get this joy and peace?

The answer can be found in the theology of shalom in the Old Testament; it is God's undeserved gift. It can be received only through humble prayer, in a spirit of gratitude, and it can remain only with those who are ready to promote peace. Christian hope does not emanate from man's heart or mind. However, there is already an investment of hope on earth; all that is good, right, just, honest and beautiful from the past represents man's cooperation with and response to God's undeserved gift. He has given us His promises and we should open-mindedly look about

91

and try to find Christ in all things, for all things are made by Him and for Him.

Finally, it is Christ Himself we are seeking, the fullness of peace and joy. But the initiative is God's, and this point is paramount in a theology of hope. We shall always experience frustration and tensions if we rely solely on our own initiative. Nevertheless, we have to acknowledge man's special way of honouring God's graciousness; man will be creative, spontaneous and generous, but the basis of man's creativity lies in his awareness of God's initiative, and his joy will then stem from his loving response to God's loving advances.

Chapter 10

HOPE AND RESPONSIBILITY
FOR THE WORLD

God has never left man without hope. However the genuine, all-embracing character of hope, the gift of the one Father of all, has often been obscured by various side-streams of religious thought. This is true within Christianity and even more so outside it. One instance would be hope as understood by *Hinayana* or "small boat" Buddhism where hope meant escaping the wheel of life by withdrawal from society. The Buddhists of this school renounced the desires and promises of this world and longed for Nirvana, *i.e.*, the final beatitude attained through the extinction of all desires. Buddhist monks and nuns of the Hinayana were highly individualistic; they wanted to save themselves personally on the small boat of the negation of life. A turn in the history of Buddhism introduces the Bodhisattva, a being that compassionately refrains from entering nirvana in order to save others. This form of Buddhism can be looked upon as somehow foreshadowing salvation in Christ.

According to Buddhist lore, the Bodhisattva first embarked on the small boat of salvation, renouncing all the desires of life and did so in perfect sincerity. However, when he arrived at the doors of nirvana and stood there about to enter, he realized that he was confronting the fullness of life, community and love. On this basis he bids God not to let him enter but rather to send him back to his brethren to bring them the message that life is not mere negation; life is actually fullness in brotherhood. So he embarked on the big boat (*Mahayana* Buddhism) which connotes concern for the salvation of all. This hymn portends Christ in a way very similar to the poems of Isaiah (Ch. 40 ff.). In the Bodhisattva we can detect the finger of God singling out and sending religious men to open up horizons of hope.

Within every religion we find people tempted to escape from the heat of the day and the turmoils of life; they want to save their souls "on the small boat" and embark on a course of religious individualism. Even Christianity has known similar side-streams contaminating the disciples of Christ, such as Manichaeism, Gnosticism and Parseeism. Each of these cults was marked by a quest for self-fulfilment or an individualistic personalism incapable of leading to the fullness of life. Complete self-realization comes only through openness to the totality of God's work and an authentic faith in the Saviour of the world.

Christ fulfilled Deutero-Isaiah's prophecy about the Servant Messiah. Christ neither eludes His brethren nor shuns their problems; on the contrary, He comes to them as the Word Incarnate. He lives a common life and shares the burden of all mankind; He bears the heat of the day until death. He is not a Saviour of disincarnate souls as the Gnostics would have it; He is the Saviour of the world, of man in his wholeness and man in his world. His message is other-worldly, freeing man from this-worldly pride and worry but sending him into this world as a messenger of peace and justice. He proclaims a new way of life which is beyond the sinful world, but there is no way to reach out for eternal life except through love of men. The big boat on which He embarks with His disciples is that of service to the hungry, the needy, the blind, the lame and the imprisoned. His Sermon on the Mount calls for brotherliness in the world and the spirit of the poor, that is, acknowledgment that all God's gifts come from the Father and therefore serve as an appeal to us to share with everybody including our enemies. If the initial call to faith reminds us of what is most precious, salvation or eternal life, it must logically become a saving sign for this world. Those who have committed themselves to the hope of everlasting life must work to strengthen all worthy earthly hopes: hope of justice, goodness, mercy, peace, brotherhood and so on.

Apart from Christ, the Christian cannot embark on the "big boat", the saving boat of hope for the present and the world to come. The reality of salvation rests in the promise of Christ who reveals the Father to us. To know Him and the Father and through Him to know how the Father loves the world is salvation for whoever knows Him and unites himself to Him for loving service of the brethren. Christ lives and dies for the glory of His Father, but He translates His devotion by a passionate concern for man and his world. Christ came to manifest the full extent and full depth of the Father's love for the created universe. His obedience to the Father's design makes Him the bread of life for the world; He even offers His body and blood for it. The incarnation, death and resurrection of Christ constitute the greatest investment in hope ever known, and manifest the nearness of the Emmanuel to His human brethren. Christ remains particularly close to those for whom the proud and self-righteous world offers little hope.

When the Christian sets sail on the big boat of brotherhood in this world, he sets out for new horizons, eternal life in the community of saints and the concelebration of God's triune love. He realizes that it is only on the big boat of solidarity with Christ that he can attain his goal because he believes in Christ, the Saviour of man who is concerned for him and his world.

Christ's mission embraces the whole created universe, the entire world in which man lives. He is the life and light of the world. "God loved the world so much that He gave His only Son . . . It was not to judge the world that God sent His Son into the world, but that through Him the world might be saved" (Jn 3: 16-17). Only in some very specific contexts of the New Testament is the word "world" used in a pejorative sense, as in the Gospel of John (17: 9), where Jesus says "I am not praying for the world but for those whom Thou hast given me"; here it is a "sacred" world that has become godless instead of opening itself to the saving solidarity and unity in Christ. The "godless world" of the Gospel of John are those men of the religious establishment who built up their comfortable nook of limited religious concern and who even used "religion" instrumentally for their career, their own pride, vanity and power. This same danger arises over and over again. We might call "unholy unworldliness" what in the Bible is called "godless world". Such people are also unconcerned for the poor and are oblivious of the prophetic tradition related to concern for orphans, widows, aliens or strangers. They form an artificial and godless world of their own because they do not share God's love for the real world.

The whole universe called into being by the creative Word senses somehow the presence of the saving Word. Hence citizens of the frustrated world still yearn and groan inwardly for hope in saving solidarity. All who are tainted by vanity or affected by the domineering attitude of Adam and Eve, all who suffer in the pernicious solidarity of oppressive power-structures, implicitly bid the disciples of Christ to relieve their misery by bringing them a share in the freedom of the sons and daughters of God. They long for "salvation" while crying out for a more just and more humane world. Without yet knowing Christ as the giver of everlasting life, they express their hope in Him through their desire of justice not only for themselves but for the whole world. Those who are visibly on the way to greater liberation from selfish individualism and group egotism, who are sailing on the "big boat" of salvation for all, are truly signs of hope for the world. Their concern for man in his daily needs and their peaceful struggle for a healthier world can open the eyes of all men of good will to the greater hope of eternal life. Their solicitude becomes all the more convincing because this very hope inspires commitment to a better world.

St. Paul develops the same theme in his own way: "There is no condemnation for those who are united with Christ Jesus, because in Christ Jesus the life-giving law of the Spirit has set you free from the law of sin and death. What the law could never do because our selfish self robbed it of all potency, God has done: by sending His own Son in a form like that of our sinful nature, and as a sacrifice for sin, He has passed judgment against sin within that very nature, so that the commandment of the law may find fulfilment in us, whose conduct, no longer under the control of our lower nature, is directed by the Spirit" (Rom 8:1-4). Paul also stresses the existential viewpoint: man must dedicate himself to hope by opening himself to the new perspective which is the absolute condition for becoming a sign of hope for the world. "Those who live on the level of the selfish nature have their outlook formed by it, and that spells death; but those who live on the level of the Spirit have the spiritual outlook, and that is life and peace. For the outlook of the selfish nature is enmity with God; it is not subject to the law of God; indeed it cannot be: those who live on such a level cannot possibly please God" (Rom 8:5-8).

Paul trusts that God's grace will set free the true self in man and conquer selfishness: "But that is not how you live. You are on the spiritual level, if only God's Spirit dwells within you; and if a man does not possess the Spirit of Christ, he is no Christian. But if Christ is dwelling within you, then although the body is a dead thing because you sinned, yet the spirit is life itself because you have been justified. Moreover, if the Spirit of Him who raised Jesus from the dead dwells within you, then the God who raised Christ Jesus from the dead will also give new life to your mortal bodies through His indwelling Spirit" (Rom 8:9-11). The new outlook that initiates saving relationships already manifests its saving power here on earth and thus strengthens the hope of resurrection. The Gospel's freedom through docility to the Spirit is also the Gospel's solidarity of the sons of God in Christ.

"For all who are moved by the Spirit of God are sons of God. The Spirit you have received is not a spirit of slavery leading you back into a life of fear, but a Spirit that makes us sons, enabling us to cry 'Abba, Father!' In that cry the Spirit of God joins with our spirit in testifying that we are God's children; and if children, then heirs. We are God's heirs and Christ's fellow-heirs, if we share his sufferings now in order to share his splendour hereafter" (Rom 8:14-17). Through the gift of the Spirit, the necessity to suffer in this world is no longer merely a frustrated sharing but a redeeming and saving one for the life of the world. Christ's suffering brings hope to

G

the whole world in all and through all who, under the law of grace, dedicate themselves for the salvation of the world.

The liberating power of solidarity in Christ through His Spirit opens up new horizons for temporal hope but they are not restricted to temporal and this-worldly hopes; they are synchronized with or integrated into the greater vision of Christian hope. "For I reckon that the sufferings we now endure bear no comparison with the splendour, as yet unrevealed, which is in store for us. For the created universe waits with eager expectation for God's sons to be revealed. It was made the victim of frustration, not by its own choice, but because of him who made it so" (Rom 8: 18-20). This text can be translated and explained in a number of different ways: the "who made it so" can be Adam, the sinner, and the collectivity of sinners, the "collective Adam" who subjects the created universe to frustration. It can also be explained in the following way, and I think this is the right explanation: God created everything with a view to solidarity and if man opts for a selfish, sinful and frustrating outlook on life, then by necessity he contaminates the world about him; he becomes a centre of frustration for the world because God created the whole world for solidarity. If by his life man does not cry "Abba, Father" in brotherhood, then by necessity he is radiating frustration about him. "Yet always there was hope, because the universe itself is to be freed from the shackles of mortality and enter upon the liberty and splendour of the children of God" (Rom 8: 21). If sin has a cosmic dimension, all the more does salvation embrace the whole universe. We can expect to find evidence of kindness, joy, hope, goodness, peace and reconciliation in the world around the true children of God. This is the vision proposed by Paul's Gospel of hope. It is not that other-worldliness of alienation of which Karl Marx accused selfish and individualistic Christians. According to Paul, the outcry of adoration, the Magnificat for God's grace means dedication as in the case of Mary, the handmaid, who remained forever vigilant for the needs of people.

"Up to the present, we know, the whole created universe groans in all its parts as if in the pangs of childbirth" (Rom 8: 22). Today particularly we can understand the meaning of

Paul's text; the secular world and the Church herself, including many religious congregations, are still moaning in labour pains. Since only hope imparts meaning to the pangs of childbirth, those who yield to pessimism and waste time in futile lamentations are really aborting the child. Christ-like hope is tested by tensions, conflicts and suffering. On the contrary, those who agree to pay the price for joy in hope are actually pioneering a new age. Salvation is operative in that hope because it is marked by the Paschal Mystery. Christ frees us from the illusions of individualistic hope. Growing pains become signs of hope when believers succeed in synthesizing renewal, understood as personal conversion, and a common effort for building a better *milieu*. Salvation becomes visible in that community of faith and hope which cares effectively for a healthier world in which to live. The created universe, the whole world around us, is frustrated by all the various conflicting structures and superstructures of selfishness, power and individualism. It groans and yearns for God's wisdom to manifest itself more powerfully. The redeemed want the new age of redemption to prevail in the history of mankind and thus to witness to hope in everlasting life. Salvation cannot be divorced from responsibility to the world. Our hopes are bound up with the destiny of the world in which we live.

The outcry of the created universe can serve our best interest, and we should listen to it if we want to live in hope. "Not only so, but even we, to whom the Spirit is given as first fruits of the harvest to come, are groaning inwardly while we wait for God to make us His sons and set our whole body free. For we have been saved, though only in hope. Now to see is no longer to hope: why should a man endure and wait for what he already sees? But if we hope for something we do not see, then, in waiting for it, we show our endurance" (Rom 8:23-25).

Salvation through the process of hope begets endurance in solidarity. Those who have come to appreciate fully how they have been saved by hope, take upon themselves the burdens of their communities as well as the tradition and burdens of the Church. However, this is only possible by paying hope-filled attention to the goodness, truth and example of the saints which is nothing less than an investment of Christ's redemptive love in the world. Only with hope and gratitude can we assume the burdens of the so-called "old world" in the Church and over-come its debilitating effects. The Church will then realize better her own solidarity with the whole world. One of the great themes of today's theology has become: how to relate the world to come, everlasting life, our hope of seeing God face to face, with present reality and with our actual joys, fears and hopes.

Christian hope is a talent or a gift of God entrusted to His disciples, an investment for the reconciliation of the world around them, the world in which they live. The talent is com-mitted to their care so that they may become signs of hope for the world. Without gratitude, however, the gift can be lost. Gratefulness expresses itself when the talent is used to generate any kind of positive element of hope for our world, for God's world. Gratitude for both the promise and the gift we have re-ceived means active hope, *i.e.*, hope-at-work taking advantage of all real opportunities to save the world, recognizing them as such and responding to the *kairos*, the time of favour or present opportunities. Hope and gratitude enable us to respond to the yearning of the world around us, to have a share in the first fruits of the free sons and daughters of God, and to be freed from selfishness and narrowness. Thus Christian life means commitment to and celebration of gratitude in hope, a celebra-tion before God and in one's daily work.

We can equally say that Christian life means celebration of hope in gratitude and celebration of gratitude in hope. It always implies a commitment to the world around us. The Christian celebration of gratitude and hope is impossible without an active commitment to redemption in response to the groaning of the world, that is, the desires of the world to have a share in the freedom of the sons and daughters of God.

The Christian has placed his hope in the one God, the one Father, the one Creator of all things, and in the one Redeemer of the world who gives Himself as the Bread "for the life of the world" (Jn 6:51). He has hope, faith and trust in the one Spirit who renews the face of the earth. The Christian sees the opposing powers of darkness but the believer knows in faith that the dark powers will not prevail; however, he will be on the side of the victor only if he bears the burden, the heat of the day according to the measure of the gifts he has received. What we are hoping for is the community of saints, the perfect brotherhood in the new earth and the new heaven. This hope inspires and quickens meaningful solidarity with all men and all creatures: political, social, economic, cultural and every kind of solidarity. If we one day discover other personal creatures on other planets, we must seek solidarity with them, because they too are made by God's Word and for Christ.

Christian hope does not look for beatitudes of a romantic I-Thou type but is a sharing or concelebration of God's redeeming and gladdening love. Life is a pilgrim situation; only through faithful solidarity with the expectations of all men and all creatures we can be on the way to final sharing and concelebration. Although we are sinners we have hope because of the gladdening news of reconciliation. We hope for the fullness of joy and peace. Therefore true believers will make a constant investment in hope, optimism, forgiveness, peace and reconciliation out of a sense of responsibility for God's world. The hope and joy, love and faith in the gladdening news must be incarnate on the soil of human history since it is proclaimed by the Word Incarnate who lived the common life of people while expressing a saving concern for all men around Him.

The pharisees and priests who did not believe in a servant Messiah wanted pure signs of power. The signs which Christ gives, on the contrary, are expressions of a healing love and a testimony of responsibility for the real needs of people. They satisfy man's temporal hopes in awakening hope for final salvation.

We hope for the new earth and the new heaven. We know that in the final analysis, only God's radiating and transforming power will bring us this new earth and new heaven. However, in the Word Incarnate who calls us to be sharers of His redeeming love for the world, God calls us to renew the earth by making a new investment in hope, justice, goodness, mercy and peace. Consequently, our hope cannot be genuine unless we actively express our faith that in the Incarnation of God's Word

101

the redemption of the earth has already begun. This is a seed entrusted to those who know that they are saved by a hope corresponding to the yearning of the world to be freed from the slavery of sin. The dogma of the Incarnation does not allow us to be content with a lazy apocalyptic hope, waiting as it were in a watchtower of dreams for the day and hour of the Lord's coming and thus escaping from any daily responsibilities. Eschatological hope in the biblical sense means a dynamic hope and active commitment to the world here and now in view of the final hope.

The messianic peace is an undeserved gift and equally undeserved promise of the final fullness of peace and joy. But only those accept and honour this gift who commit themselves here and now to the order of peace. The unselfishness, purity of intention and energy of hope with which believers commit themselves to peace on earth, to justice and human development, and to the unity and solidarity of all men, is the best indication of and witness to the full scope of the messianic peace.

We should not overlook the fact however, that there can be genuine responsibility for the world inspired by a firm hope for human history alone, a hope manifesting itself in solidarity and justice without any explicit hope of eternal life. The patriarchs of Israel probably had great hope of future peace on earth before they came to a full vision of eternal life and the resurrection of the individual person. But as their trust in God, their experience with His covenant and their feeling of a call to solidarity in the covenant grew, their hopes were projected to horizons beyond Israel and beyond this earthly life.

Talk about "anonymous Christians" can give the impression that those who do not know Christ have generally a Christlike love. But everyone can see that this is not the case. When confronted with Christ's saving love, so much of what the world calls love is unmasked as a lie. The same holds true of many forms of temporal hope.

There are forms of hope which betray man's pride, his foolish trust in himself, in technical progress, power and so on. The hope God offers in His covenant to man is often built on the breakdown of such arrogant hopes. Nevertheless, as I have indicated earlier, there are genuine forms of temporal hope such as a commitment to peace, dedication to racial reconciliation and social justice; it is the hope that the dignity of each person will be respected. This kind of hope is a precious talent entrusted by God to man. Wherever this talent is put to good use through God's presence, mankind comes closer to God's promise for this age and for the world to come.

Human hope, trust, optimism and perseverance in the commitment to a better future can reflect the fullness of eschatological hope. They can have the quality of an *analogia spei,* that is, a hidden presence, an initial manifestation of ever greater hope, a reality longing for an ever greater God and pointing to trust in Him. Whatever is good and right in temporal hope, in mutual trust and dedication to the future of others, is already quickened by the same God who gives the fullness of His promise in Jesus Christ. As long as man transcends himself and opens himself to the common future of all in hope, we have hopeful degress of consciousness pointing towards that hope in Christ in which all the dimensions of man's calling come into play.

We need to look at the whole experience of temporal hope in order to get a vital picture of the hope to which Christ calls us. For instance, we notice that in difficult situations strong men tend to fade away as soon as they have given up hope. On the other hand, we know how weak bodies reacted to similarly trying situations in jail and in prison camps because these persons did not abandon hope for a single moment; very often their hope was sustained by the trust shown them by beloved persons. We know how a difficult or seemingly ungifted child can be helped to develop if he is shown trust and given credit in a convincing way. On the other hand, if a doctor, analyst or confessor informs a neurotic person that he even lacks the freedom to commit a venial sin, he destroys all hope and thwarts all efforts which could have been inspired by more patient encouragement and understanding.

We know from our experience with human hope in daily life that a person cannot preserve and strengthen his hope without making an appropriate effort to obtain the things hoped for. By a persistent and prudent effort to obtain worthwhile things with a firm attitude of hope, we prepare people for a better understanding of the dynamism of Christian hope.

Our dynamic culture today provides daily proof that those who become self-complacent, in economic or in professional life or in politics, are headed for failure and pessimism. We should accept this as a warning against any static perspective with respect to Christian life and hope. Hope lives and grows when the whole life of the Church and of the person is seen as a constant process of renewal, as a continuous conversion and a tireless striving. Hope exists when the pilgrim Church and each individual person knows and is fully aware that on earth love can never be perfect but is forever growing in response to God's call: "Be all goodness just as your heavenly Father is all good" (Mt 5:48). The realization that all human achievements are an unfinished task can serve as a strong impetus to a vital understanding of Christian hope.

Partial failures are the lot of man; they can even arouse him to exert new energies provided man does not give up hope. Experience here sheds light on an important aspect of the Gospel of reconciliation. The sinner, turning more decidedly towards God and awakening to greater vigilance and unceasing prayer, realizes that God can write straight with crooked lines.

Quite often acceptance of one's responsibilities in the temporal realm can entail disquiet, conflict and contradiction. However, men of hope mature in the most difficult moments of life. If these experiences are seen in the light of faith, we realize better that suffering and conflict accepted in Christ can lead to perseverance and render hope more stable.

Chapter 11

MAN'S BODY IN THE LIGHT OF HOPE

Man yearns for salvation in his wholeness and not just for the saving of a soul separated from his body. The great Greek philosophers were convinced they could prove the immortality of man's spiritual soul, and thus the Hellenistic world providentially paved the way for the proclamation of the Gospel of eternal life. I believe that God had prepared this culture by enlightening man to realize his inner potential and demonstrate intellectually that man's spiritual part transcends this mortal life. However there were severe limitations on Greek belief in the immortality of the soul. Some trends, such as Platonism, conceived man's body as a prison for the soul; this negative attitude was further strengthened by Gnosticism, Manichaeism and similar religious views originating in Asia, particularly in Persia.

The religion of Zarathustra taught that Ahura Mazda, the god of light and wisdom, created man's soul, the angels (pure spirits) and ideas, whereas Ahriman, the god of darkness, was responsible for man's body and the visible material world. Zoroastrianism is a seductive religion in the sense that it leads to an escapism of a purely inactive theoretical type; its type of contemplation justifies non-involvement or non-commitment with respect to the visible world. The Bible adopts a firm stand on this point. In the first Epistle of St. John, those persons who deny the goodness of the body and of the material world are referred to as "godless world" because they fail to acknowledge God's presence in our body and in His world. Such people try to manoeuvre God out of this world, out of marriage, out of economic life and out of politics. They deny God the honour we can and must render Him in our bodies. The Bible emphatically teaches that the body is the temple of the Holy Spirit and not a prison for the soul.

While hailing the progress of an age that believed in the immortality of the soul, the Christian message sought to correct and complete this notion; what we are hoping for is the resurrection, the full liberation of the visible person: "We believe in the resurrection of the body." This is the central message of the Paschal Mystery, of the death and resurrection of Christ; it is an assurance that we are created and redeemed for eternal life in the wholeness of the body and spirit. It commits us to the visible world where God has appeared visibly in the Word Incarnate, His Son, and it commits us very positively to glorify God in our body.

The theology of both Old and New Testaments envisages the visible world, including man's body, as a reflection of the glory of God, that is, His wisdom and majesty; in the body God's creative love dynamically shines through, bringing joy, gratitude and trust to man. The human body manifesting trust, joy, peace, goodness and gentleness praises God and serves as an invitation to hope. The Bible very often refers to the image of countenance, e.g., "cháris", grace; this means the gracious countenance of God, God turning His countenance to man and thus inspiring him with hope and trust. God has truly graced us in His visible image, Jesus Christ, radiant with goodness, with mercy and patience. It is in union with Christ, therefore, and through Christ that man's body, man's countenance, can be above all, a sign of hope, and can radiate goodness, gentleness, kindness, purity, reverence, loving care and compassion.

Man's hand was ingeniously fashioned to use tools and instruments, but the hand can also be a sign, a symbol of communication and of joining together in trust and friendship. Man's turning his whole body to another in reverence thus becomes a visible image of God who is close to man and imparts dignity to His creatures.

Great concern must be shown for man's physical and mental health. I have always been impressed on my visits to Africa by the tremendous work being done by the nuns caring for the sick. Arriving at a dispensary in the morning, I would see 50 to 150 weak people awaiting the ministrations of the one sister-nurse who was also training two or three helpers. The missionaries' great contribution to the fight against malnutrition is surely a great sign of hope, because faulty and inadequate diets so often cause blindness and other serious defects. From the very beginning the Church has followed Christ's lead in its concern for health; it is one of the achievements of Christian civilization to care for the sick, attending as Christ did, to sick bodies, and today paying more attention yet to psychological health.

Health should not become an idol, but health and life should be viewed in the light of the Paschal Mystery. The greatest strength is found in people who forget themselves to serve relatives and friends in need, who day after day devote themselves to the service of others instead of ruining their health with unfounded worries about themselves. Christ truly devoted His life to generous service of His brethren: "Behold, O Lord, thou has prepared Me a body; I come to do Thy will" (Heb 10: 5-7). This is the morning prayer of Christ's entire life. His last breath glorifies the Father as He hands over to Him His body for the salvation of the world.

Sexuality, a healthy dimension of man's life, also has to be seen in this light. We have no difficulty today in accepting as a probable hypothesis the idea that man is intimately linked to the entire physical universe and especially the world of living things. Through evolution and the marvellous progress of life, God prepared the human body and breathed spiritual life into it. Although man has sexual powers in common with the higher animals, his sexuality transcends theirs by far. It becomes a language, a conscious communication of love, each to the other, as well as a creative transmission of life.

We find a marvellous image of the creative love and power of God even in the sexuality of animals. There is more than bare instrumentality here; there is great joy and tenderness, a protective concern, although consciousness is lacking. But in the total process of evolution the life of animals can be considered as a promise of man's more highly developed sexuality. In man, sexuality becomes a conscious manifestation of love, dedication and commitment to a greater vocation. It calls for a covenant of persons who, in their spiritual unity, must not deprecate bodily and sexual expression of love where their covenant benefits by it.

Among animals one finds a drive in mating partners to associate for the rearing of offspring; we already have a tentative design but in man this becomes a reality. However, man must invest with a conscious effort in this direction. If man is prepared to live truly in the totality of human hope, sexuality can be transfigured. It befits the dignity of a person who lives in freedom and responsibility and affects all of his energy in the total vocation of love. I am not referring solely to that transfiguration of human sexuality in those persons called to celibacy for the heavenly kingdom, where all the energies and passions are brought home joyfully to the Lord and concentrated on unselfish dedication and love in the service of mankind. Such a life is transformed into compassionate love for the needy; the life style itself becomes a message, a gospel of eternal hope. I am alluding also to the transfiguration of sexuality in marriage when it is consecrated by a sacrament and where, through the presence of God's creative and redeeming love, it then becomes a communication of and dedication to an irrevocable covenant of love.

St. Gregory Nazianzen similarly refers to the transfigured sexuality of marriage in the beautiful poem he sang at the funeral of his mother. Through her tender bodily union she had brought her husband to the unity in one Spirit. Prior to his marriage, Gregory's father had been an unbeliever, but he had come to faith in God's love through the tender love of his wife. As early as the fourth century, then, reference was made in this connection to the great vision of the Transfiguration. Man's sexuality cannot and should not be reduced to the mere instrumental value of procreation.

In the vision of the Bible, the sexual union of the spouses is understood as a mutual knowing; in this way man and wife communicate to each other what they are and what they wish to become as they grow in love. Quite different is the stark reality of those who use their sexuality for the purpose of selfish gratification and to degrade and exploit others. In such cases, sexuality is a reality to be redeemed. A sign of redemption and hope is offered such people in the total witness of those who freely choose celibacy for the heavenly kingdom as well as that of the truly married who consecrate themselves faithfully to mutual growth in love and maturity within their great vocation as spouses and parents. Both in celibacy and in marriage, a truly transfigured sexuality entails a continuous effort to devote one's energies, passions and sexuality to the full communication of dedicated, tender and respectful love in view of the final hope of fulfilment in the resurrection.

The married and the celibate therefore have never fully completed their task; their commitment is both a promise and a hopeful beginning. There remains the constant task for them to transform sexuality more and more, in the spirit of the Transfiguration, of making it more and more a message of unselfish love according to the various charisms which people have received. It is one of the glories of Catholic doctrine that contrary to all tendencies towards degrading the body and particularly sexuality, the Church has consistently upheld marriage as a sacrament. The essence of its sacramentality consists in the fact that two persons become one body in the totality of their bodily union and their life together. Disintegration sets in when one partner wants sexual union without the totality of sharing his life and dedication.

Man's body receives the highest valuation through the dogma of the resurrection of the body. In the Eucharist we enter into a mystical union with the risen body of the Lord. Christ's body is marked by His wounds and by all the sufferings borne in His body for the sake of His brothers and sisters. His body uniquely manifests the glory of the Father, since through it, in the course of His life and particularly in His death, there shines forth the love of the Father for all men. Thus, the body has become a great sacrament, a visible sign of the most spiritual kind of love.

Through our union with Christ, all hard work, physical and mental suffering as well as every expression of tender love becomes a visible sign of hope and resurrection. In the risen body of each person there will be fully and eternally visible everything he has done for the glory of God and out of love for his fellowman during his bodily life. The risen body lies at the heart of the new heaven and new earth. Already here on earth, the grace of God received in gratitude becomes somehow visible in the graciousness and gentleness of a person. The beauty radiated by the innermost goodness of a person is a sign of hope. Its meaning can be fully appreciated in the light of faith in the resurrection of the body.

For the unbeliever death means the destruction of man's body. For the believer it means the final "yes" to God's will, the final union with Christ by acceptance of death as a most decisive manifestation of trust in God, and of redeemed and redeeming love for all mankind. So death is the greatest, the ultimate sign of hope.

Chapter 12

NATURAL LAW AND HOPE

There is no consensus, either within the Church or outside it, about what is meant by natural law. The Stoic and Aristotelian philosophers began with the common ground of man and animal; in other words, they based their ideas about natural law on the biological-physiological make-up of man. Moralists who adopted this mistaken approach considered prostitution and fornication sins *according to* man's nature whereas masturbation was held to be a sign *against* nature. Their reasoning was that fornication accorded with the natural course of sexuality while masturbation was unnatural; consequently, masturbation was a more serious offense. The great convert from the Russian Orthodox Church, Vladimir Soloviov, who in my eyes is one of the greatest theologians of all times, makes great fun of this vision of natural law. How can it be natural for a man to want the body of another person just to abuse it? He likens this to necrophilia, the love of dead bodies, where a man desires a corpse and not a person; this is wholly unnatural for the human person.

If we wish to speak about nature, we have to begin with man's true personality, his openness to God, to the Thou and the We. Then the significance of the body can be seen in proper perspective. A person who is able to communicate faithfully and respectfully will necessarily want to share his experiences and thoughts, reflecting together with his fellowman on where he came from and where he is going, on his origin and his destiny.

111

A variety of perspectives on natural law has emerged in the course of history; of necessity, I can consider here only a few. The one that has probably exerted the greatest influence on us is the viewpoint elaborated by Roman lawyers. Their intention was chiefly political: to maintain dominance over the various tribes and nations conquered in the course of their many wars. They compared the different tribal and national traditions and teased out the common elements. Their formulation of natural law therefore emerged from a comparative study of cultures not so much for the sake of assuring man's dignity as for the maintenance of their own power. They spoke of a *Pax Romana*, the Roman Peace, when it was nothing other than a matter of keeping all the conquered peoples subject to their dominion. The Romans were shrewd and prudent politicians who sought to impose on the whole empire only what the various groups had in common, what could be imposed on all tribes without driving them to rebellion. However, their wisdom was mainly or essentially political and bore the stamp of original sin, namely the desire to domineer. The natural law of the Romans symbolizes the establishment, any establishment. The hope it held out was one of order through political submission, and acceptance of two classes of people, Roman citizen and non-citizen.

Another approach to natural law that has greatly influenced the course of our own history is that of the Greeks. Their views on natural law began to evolve into a theory when the different Greek-speaking cities came to know each other better through greater navigation and entered into a somewhat loose confederation. It was a civilization comprised of city-states of similar cultural backgrounds that joined in a free alliance. The basic difference from the Romans was that the Greeks wished to exchange their experiences and products in freedom with mutual respect while enriching each other.

Imperial policy came into the picture when Alexander the Great conquered Egypt and the greater part of western Asia. With the eventual fusion of cultures, independently of politicians there developed a new cosmopolitan outlook characteristic of the Hellenistic age. No longer did thinkers consider themselves citizens of a city-state marked by narrowness of political ambi-

112

tions; they wanted to be citizens of the world. The age witnessed a tremendous broadening of world vision, the outcome of an extraordinary enrichment resulting from so many cultures entering into dialogue and communicating with each other freely and respectfully. However when compared to our present situation, the world of the Greeks was a very small world. Unfortunately, moreover, most people uncritically accepted the prevailing distinction between free men and slaves, and considered women as inferior beings.

Similarly we find very interesting and attractive developments in the writings of Confucius at a time when many cultural trends were blending together in China and sharing experiences and insights. Those who formulated Chinese ethical theories were pedagogues and not primarily politicians. They drew on all the experiences and reflections of the various interacting cultures without intending to establish any political domination. I am very fond of the four Holy Books of Confucius; they contain a great wealth of wisdom and constitute a wonderful testimony to a highly developed culture. For instance, when Confucius describes the four cardinal virtues he does not refer to them as "virtues". For the Aristotelians and Stoics the political outlook is still dominant; they present virtue as self-perfection and a male prerogative; self-fulfilment was the *leitmotiv*. Confucius, on the other hand, speaks of "the four greatest gifts heaven has bestowed upon man." There is a world of difference between "heaven has bestowed" and "my four greatest achievements". The order in which Confucius mentions the heavenly gifts is: benevolence or kindness, gentleness, wisdom and justice. Benevolence or kindness is profoundly described as man's innermost being turned respectfully towards his neighbour; it is a capacity of man's heart and of man's being to love and to serve. Gentleness is described with reference to China's old fondness for the mirror; men and women would look into the mirror to see if they were happy or sad, refined or uncouth. Confucius insisted that we cannot learn gentleness before the mirror; this virtue demands benevolence towards others and a deep respect for the community. Gentleness is the natural manifestation of the splendour of man's heart; if his mind is respectful and be-

H

nevolent, it will be reflected in the eyes, mouth, hands and in the whole countenance of the person. Gentleness, then, is understood as the communication of kindness and love. In the Chinese version of natural law we have a great vision which comes close to that of the Bible; it is not a theory based on power or politics but on the most fundamental human experiences.

In Greek philosophical-ethical systems, we notice the absence of love and kindness in the cardinal virtues; "political" prudence remains in the foreground. The Stoics maintained that love was a passion and as such had to be eliminated. Later, Immanuel Kant improved on Greek pessimism by asserting that love was a pathological affair, *"eine pathologische Angelegenheit"*. Allow me, however, to add a good word in favour of my compatriot; he did have lucid moments, and in one of these he stated that the three greatest gifts which heaven has granted man in compensation for human miseries are: sound sleep, a smile or laughter, and hope. Kant's natural law ethics, unfortunately, is too one-sided, dominated as it is by the concept of duty (*Pflicht*).

We may legitimately ask what natural law means for us today, or what it should mean? Naturally, it should include a readiness to learn from all earlier ethical schools, but we must realize that before systems of philosophy were elaborated there was already an accumulated wealth of human experience and shared insights. This found expression in many collections of wisdom and proverbs, in the experiences of people living together in community and in persons who were able to share their experiences and their reflections. So natural law is fundamentally humanity on the march, constantly seeking to achieve a better understanding of man's place in the world and in life. It is definitely not a closed philosophical system enshrined in a fossilized terminology. It is simply unnatural for man to feel self-satisfied and close-minded about his search for what is morally good; he cannot limit himself to the mere repetition of earlier formulations. What is natural to man throughout history is openness to God's intention that humanity develop and grow in breadth and depth. There are today increasing opportunities favouring the sharing of experiences and insights; our vast communications networks suggest and foster the idea of co-operation on all levels. In turn, these achievements help us to grasp the meaning of abiding truth in greater depth and increase our capacity to discern the changing forms of truth and to isolate its essence. Man's historical and social nature requires a constant openness to God, to new experiences and to improved means of sharing experiences and reflection. Man is called to live in community; he cannot live in isolation as an abstract thinker; by his nature, man is destined to be an outgoing person, sensing and responding to goodness and kindness, suffering from injustice, sharing kindness and understanding; in short, man is to be a learner.

The basic element of the law written in man's heart is the Golden Rule as expressed in the book of Tobit (4: 15): "Do not do to others what you would not want them to do to you" or as expressed more positively in the Sermon on the Mount: "Always treat others as you would like them to treat you" (Mt 7: 12). Only when people come to believe in one God, Creator and Father of all men, is this law properly understood and practised with great spontaneity. However we find it in a more or less limited way in the course of the evolution of cultures. Consider, for example, the tremendous difference between the Ice Age or Stone Age in terms of outlook and that of the present age of jumbo-jet planes and television!

In earlier periods people belonging to certain castes regarded only members of their own class as fellowmen; only in exceptional cases did they come to realize that people from other castes were neighbours needing help or capable of giving help. In other older cultures we find the institution of "blood brotherhood"; when two tribes came to realize that they could live in friendship and were neighbours who needed one another, they made a "blood covenant". This consisted in the symbolic transfusion of blood from one person to another thus indicating a blood relationship.

Progress came about as time moved on. Among most African tribes, the receiving of hospitality was looked upon as a sign of religion; it had to do with belief in the one Creator of all men. The Jewish prophets made it a great sign of genuine

115

religion for widows, orphans and aliens, men from other nations, to be treated as guests. They were regarded as standing symbolically for all who could not remunerate money-wise or return the kindness. The gesture ascribed equal dignity to all men. Man's very nature thus visibly calls for mutual respect, love and help.

At a critical moment of this learning process, in order to broaden our vision about our "neighbour", Christ tells us the story of the merciful Samaritan. The priest and the Levite, over-concerned with formalism and rubricism, did not recognize the wounded man of their own nation as their neighbour. But the Samaritan, a man from a schismatic and heretic nation, was not a formalist; he saw him, was moved by compassion and took care of him at his own expense.

Today, the modern sciences of paleontology and archeology help us to look back at the great steps leading to humanization; ethnology and history help us to understand most past cultures; comparative cultures are studied in sociology and anthropology; new modes of communication and travel have shrunk the distances separating different cultures and enable us to share experiences in new ways. We cannot categorically exclude the dream that it may be possible for the next generation to share experiences with personal beings living on other planets who may have achieved greater progress than we have in some aspect of human development. This would certainly add a new dimension to our understanding of natural law! At any rate it is a tremendous advance of our age for people of all cultures to be in contact with each other and to be able to rid themselves gradually of the unnatural sinful attitude characteristic of so many closed nationalistic cultures which sought to impose themselves as norms on others.

If we now look over the achievements of natural law we can see great progress, as in the case of St. Thomas Aquinas, who focused his attention on the existential aspect of human experience, on the practical reason, though he was limited by the science and culture of his day. For example, Aquinas claims as a part of natural law that the human male as procreator always intends to produce male offspring; it is only by a partial failure, for some unknown reason, that a female is born. Aquinas lived in a male-ordained society and was hemmed in by the serious limitations of the views on reproductive biology, that knew only of the male sperm; scientists had no idea of the existence of the ovule. Therefore, the man was regarded as the procreator of life and the woman was thought of only as a bearer of life. This vision was a very narrow one indeed. It is obvious that the Catholic Church cannot say: "We have always known this . . .", for this is simply not true. If she says: "Since Thomas Aquinas taught this, we have to retain it" or "generations have become used to thinking in this way and the popes have consistently referred to his thought . . .", she creates a serious credibility gap.

It is natural for man to commit errors and to correct them, to learn and to unlearn. So it is "natural" for the pilgrim Church to share the limitations of a certain culture and she should be fully aware of this; as soon as new insights appear, she should be open to them. The Church should always be very sensitive to any new possibility of sharing and learning. She must not be allowed to wallow in outdated formulas; a vision of natural law is genuine if it is dynamic and filled with hope. This fact should become more evident when human experience and the human learning process come in contact with the fuller vista of hope in history in the light of eschatological hope.

An infant's progression in learning is a marvellous phenomenon; we can sometimes detect a smile as early as the first few weeks. The child has already learned from the love of his parents how to smile; this is a promising beginning. However, this quick, wonderfully simple process is only a hope that the child will reach the full maturity of wisdom, understanding and love. It is a hope, a history that calls for ever fuller awareness of the possibility and need of further development. Each man is a history, has a history, lives a history and shapes history. Humanity does not start out with a heavy baggage of formulas, propositions and systems; it sets out with a capacity to live and to learn, and to unlearn and correct experiences. But within the realm of faith, there should be even greater readiness to learn because religion is not an ideology or closed system of philosophy; it is God's history, God's ongoing word: "My Father has not yet ceased to work and I am working too" (Jn 5:17), working on ever new things. In this history of salvation, Christ provides the great orientation; Christ is the Word Incarnate and the creative word continuing human history. We must evince that great openness to "the signs of the times" so strongly recommended by Vatican II.

In *Gaudium et spes,* the Council rightly says that our contemporary world is passing from a more static to a more dynamic order. The world was never fully static but man did not always have the same awareness of the transience of life and its changing conditions. Mankind and the Church have always had the duty of scrutinizing the new signs of the times and of interpreting them. In its document on the *Church in the Modern World* the Council says: "Today, the human race is passing through a new stage of its history. Profound and rapid changes are spreading by degrees around the whole world. Triggered by the intelligence and creative energies of man, these changes recoil upon him, upon his decisions and desires, both individual and collective, and upon his manner of thinking and acting with respect to things and to people. Hence we can already speak of a true social and cultural transformation, one which has repercussions on man's religious life as well" (GS, Art. 4). Here, then, we find acknowledged the newness of the present situation. It follows that it would be quite unnatural and sinful to cling to traditional formulas and to be unwilling to open one's horizons. Thus it is natural for redeemed man to praise God for every new possibility.

The Council also helps us to face new difficulties but in a positive, optimistic way: "As happens in any crisis of growth, this transformation has brought serious difficulties in its wake" (GS, Art. 4). First there should be praise to God for all our growing pains — are they not better than the painlessness of the graveyard? "Today's spiritual agitation and the changing conditions of life are part of a broader and deeper revolution. As a result of the latter, intellectual formation is ever increasingly based on the mathematical and natural sciences and on those dealing with man himself" (GS, Art. 5). It is evident that we need to make a systematic effort to learn more about man and his being. "History itself speeds along on so rapid a course that an individual person can scarcely keep abreast of it. The destiny of the human community has become all of a piece, where once the various groups of men had a kind of private history of their own. Thus, the human race has passed from a rather static concept of reality to a more dynamic, evolutionary one. In consequence, there has arisen a new series of problems, a series as important as can be, calling for new efforts of analysis and synthesis" (GS, Art. 5). This constant openness in the sharing of experiences and co-reflection flows from natural law understood as man's nature throughout history; natural law cannot be a self-complacent repetition of old formulas. Man's nature calls for a constant revision of positions in the light of new insights provided by the behavioural and natural sciences, and as demanded by the changing conditions of today's world.

In the same pastoral constitution, the Council speaks dynamically of the concept of conscience as a searching for truth. The Catholic cannot say: we know it all; we have nothing more to learn. "In fidelity to conscience, Christians are joined with the rest of men in the search for truth, and for the genuine solution to the numerous problems which arise in the life of individuals and from social relationships" (GS, Art. 16). So conscience is dynamic and hopeful.

In article 43, the pastoral constitution states clearly that Christians should not look to their bishops for all solutions. They should not even expect the bishops to know all the answers; the whole people of God has to be in dialogue, all sharing experiences and insights with one another in order the better to resolve their difficulties. They have to accept, as a sign of hope, a variety of approaches that can correct and complete one another. Article 44 says that the Church is in dialogue with the world not only by teaching the world something but by learning from the whole of human history. This is entirely different from the concept of one curial cardinal who invited religious superiors to dialogue with the Sacred Congregation of Religious; he meant that they should turn to the Sacred Congregation with their problems because it has all the answers and is thus in a position to tell them what to do. Such a paternalistic form of "dialogue" is better termed "monologue" and is definitely not in keeping with the Council's thinking. Why could he not have said: "Inform us of your difficulties; indicate the points on which you are in disagreement with us and help us correct our views. Sisters from all over the world should have representation in the Sacred Congregation for Religious; it would enable them to apply the wealth of their experiences for the benefit of the whole Church. Everybody should feel free to speak to us in complete frankness for mutual enrichment, correction and encouragement. We know that all the congregations are searching, and our Office should serve as a centre of communication for all religious." The Council has set a very clear direction and speaks forcefully to the Church as a learner.

The view of the Council is in no way contrary to the concept of infallibility. I would explain infallibility in the Church as being, above all, an unfailing learning process. Infallibility has been defined, that is, its limits have been set. In 1870 the men in the curia wanted a blank cheque: "whatever the pope does is infallible and nobody can contradict him". A minority of bishops, however, a minority that represented almost two-thirds of the members of the Catholic Church at that time, drew up long lists of errors committed in the past. They insisted on a definition — not in the sense of a plain approval of whatever the pope and the curia do, but of a clearcut delimitation as to when the pope can be said to speak infallibly. The result was that when the pope bases his pronouncement on divine revelation and speaks as supreme teacher in urgent situations, *ex cathedra*, he binds the whole Church. This is a limitation not in the sense that the whole mystery is exhausted, but only in the sense that a limit is placed on the direction in which he can go. There always remains the necessity of constantly learning, of understanding better the mystery so as to see its different dimensions and be in a more favourable position to proclaim it in different contexts.

The bishops fully intended to exclude mere natural law insights from the 1870 definition. Before the vote was cast, Bishop Gasser explained in the name of the doctrinal commission that it had not intended to include in the definition of infallibility those theological matters not belonging directly to the deposit of faith. [1] Vatican II followed the lead of Vatican I in explaining that "this infallibility with which the divine Redeemer willed His Church to be endowed in defining a doctrine of faith and morals extends as far as the deposit of divine revelation, which must be religiously guarded and faithfully explained" (LG, Art. 25). From this it can be concluded that we do not have to believe that any infallibility is involved in a pope's statement about natural law or any single matter relating to natural law, when his teaching is not backed by the deposit of faith as revealed in Christ.

Notwithstanding, we trust that God will protect His Church and that in spite of partial failures as an unfailing community of learners, she will remain a sign of hope and trustworthy guide to salvation. God protects her in so far as she is a community of salvation on pilgrimage. Therefore, the more she is willing to learn and unlearn, to admit past errors and a partial lack of docility to His word, the more she becomes a sacrament of hope for all men of good will.

In the proceedings of the Congress of Italian Moralists that met in April, 1970, in Padua, the final document reads: "In this vision of constant learning, the role of the magisterium is to be outstanding in the art of listening and promoting dialogue; thus it will be able to speak a prophetic forward-looking word and help towards discernment." This is perfectly in line with the outlook of the Council. On all levels we come to a deeper understanding of the message of Christ which is one with the whole message God unfolds to us gradually, progressively, through the history of mankind. So it is a common search, a common striving in solidarity but also in gratitude for the great wealth of tradition. We do not discard past teaching; it has been integrated in history and we learn from it. However, we have to continue learning from God who has never ceased to

---

[1] Theodor Granderath, S.J., *Geschichte des Vatikanischen Konzils von seiner ersten Ankündigung bis zu seiner Vertagung,* Vol. III (Freiburg, 1906), p. 476.

work in the world. We have to use all the means Divine Providence places at our disposal in this scientific era. It means a common searching with a sense of responsibility towards humanity today and future generations. We capitalize on the present opportunities because they outline our duty towards generations to come. All experiences must be seen in the light of Christ and be tested against the life-giving standards of the Paschal Mystery; then all events in history can be understood as signs of God's presence and as signs of His saving judgment.

Most cultures have myths or legends about the origin of mankind. Mythological language has found a place even in the Bible. A myth conveys a profound truth, but it is expressed with the awareness that the truth itself is greater than any human formulation. Almost all nations and tribes had myths about their ancestors living originally in peace and goodness, wisdom and happiness; they then did shameful things and lived far from God. However there are great divergencies in these various myths. In some cultures mythology leads to despair and resignation because there is an exclusive turning towards the past accompanied by regret that things turned out so badly.

In biblical terminology, the myth of paradise discloses man's search for a deeper understanding of the original design of God, but in such a way that the signs of hope prevail, as the fourth Eucharistic prayer says so well: "God has never left man without hope." The lost paradise is ultimately a promise for the future because the Creator never renounces His design in spite of man's sinfulness or in spite of the possibility of temporary decay. God's promises direct man's vision towards the future; they lend meaning to each new effort, sustain our readiness to set out towards an unknown future to attain the fullness of life. This is characteristic of the outlook we find in the Bible. From this we should learn that thought about natural law is in keeping with the real nature of historical man because of hope. The order of creation and the order of redemption are parts of the same master-design of God. Any ethical system that contradicts this truth must be regarded as unnatural, and fails to grasp the vision of hope.

The dynamic view of man's nature is not limited to one

culture or one philosophy; this would bespeak a lack of fidelity to the Lord of history who works in all and through all people. It would lower the dignity of man's nature. At the present time, God has granted us unique new possibilities of encounter, dialogue and mutual enrichment. All existing cultures can take advantage of the achievements and errors of others for the benefit of future progress. This provides a new element of hope in our efforts to grasp the length and the breadth of human nature and human history.

There still remain distressing gaps between religion and life in many systems of thought and in portions of the Church. One way to span the gap is to work out a better theory of natural law in an attempt to understand better what man is, how he can progress and how he can take the next step towards greater fidelity to God and towards greater personal fulfilment. Christian hope is a great vision and perspective capable of integrating all human experiences; thus it becomes a kind of pre-evangelization, a real opportunity to maintain a lively, meaningful and mutually beneficial dialogue with men of all times.

Chapter 13

ABOUNDING IN PEACE

Earthly hopes, as long as they remain true to life and open for the ever greater hope, are a gift and sign of the peace that comes from God. All gladdening events in the secular realm, when they strengthen hope and breed open-mindedness, lead finally to Christ since they have in them their final ground and hope. But the ways of experience are many and varied. Some people need a great deal of happy earthly experiences, much encouragement and sometimes a good deal of frustration prior to the collapse of their illusions; they eventually come upon the fountain of all hope, God who in Jesus Christ meets our deepest desires. For others, the full sun of hope rises early; they promptly behold Christ, the Light and Life of the world. Far from being dazzled by this overwhelming brightness, they gradually en-visage all things and events in the light of Christ. They in turn become reflectors of light and hope; everyone coming in contact with them realizes that such persons do not consider themselves to be the source of light and peace. Their whole existence turns attention to Christ.

It is in this sense that we consider the messianic peace (shalom), the great gift of Christ in view of a new order of love and hope. Shalom, the unequalled gift of Easter Sunday, be-comes light only for the person who truly accepts it as an undeserved favour intended to inundate the world with peace. It is a gift to the individual person, but one that presses to become a stream of hope for many.

In Christian hope, we experience that God in Jesus Christ offers peace and salvation to those who entrust themselves to Him and accept their mission as messengers of hope for the world. We allow God's Word and gracious gift to become plenitude over-flowing into the fullness of peace and knowledge of Jesus Christ which transcends all knowledge (Cf. Eph 3:19). Whoever humbly and gratefully accepts the peace of Christ will realize more and more that Christ is the hope for all of mankind and the whole created universe. Whoever truly lives in faith with Christ, the peace and hope of the world, will come to understand better his own mission as one of cooperation in the redemption of all earthly hopes and manifestation of the power of the messianic peace throughout his life.

The overflowing peace of Christ manifests itself abundantly in a life according to the beatitudes and the evangelical counsels. Those persons who accept the grace of the Holy Spirit and every gift of God as their rule of life will not only experience how peacemakers are called sons and daughters of God (Mt 5:9), but will be careful to turn the attention of others to the only-begotten Son of the Father who has come to reconcile all men with God and with each other.

A life according to the evangelical counsels, of simplicity in service, humility in co-responsibility, and celibacy in growing capacity to love, is a sign of God's presence in the world and leads to openness to the needs of other men. Those who dedicate themselves totally to the victory of God's love in the world become instruments of reconciliation. It is expected that sisters, brothers and laymen who live fully according to the evangelical counsels be vigilant for the needs of the discriminated-against, the handicapped and drug-addicted, that they be ready to serve in the poor schools of the slums rather than in private schools for the upper middle class. That this is so stems from the fact that a life according to the Sermon on the Mount and in total dedication to it is destined to experience the oneness of the messianic peace and a commitment to peace and genuine human development.

One of the most outstanding examples of such dedication to hope was Brother Albert, who worked untiringly to improve the conditions of the poor. He had first been one of the great freedom fighters of Poland; in the course of a battle, he lost a leg. He later on became a famous painter. Everyone found himself at home in his *atelier* and he did not mind everyone's helping himself freely to whatever he needed. Brother Albert already had a number of "disorderly friends" when he finally decided to take up quarters in the slums of Cracow in a sector of the city so dangerous that even the police dared not penetrate. Before he settled there, Brother Albert had pleaded with the city officials not to use his presence in the slums as a reason for entering and attempting to establish control because he believed in the power of a vulnerable, peaceful presence.

Brother Albert did not believe nor did he engage in moralizing corrections. He simply wanted to be present as a brother among brethren and try to improve their housing situation. He organized plays and all kinds of wholesome recreational activities. Through his presence, the gospel of peace became more incarnate in the life of these poor people. Within one year the crime rate in Cracow had fallen by more than 50%. He had succeeded in convincing these people, until now deprived and depraved, that they needed to join forces for the improvement of their living conditions and whole environment.

Once after receiving a substantial sum of money for his work, one of his friends broke his wooden leg, robbed him and disappeared. The thought never even occurred to Brother Albert to denounce him to the police. After a few months the culprit returned; Brother Albert embraced him and said simply: "I knew you would return." Such is the power of hope and peace. It is an incarnate hope that inspires temporal hope even in hopeless situations. Brother Albert's powerful message had opened minds and hearts to a new understanding of Christian hope.

It is not to favour pessimism that I illustrate the same truth by a "skunk" story. Some twenty years ago in Bavaria, a movement called the Bavarian Party wanted to set up a big, ostentatious gambling casino that would attract wealthy people from all over the world. The vocal advocates of this gambling venture were later tried in connection with bribery charges. In any event, they marshalled every possible argument to prove to Parliament the need for such an institution: it would contribute to the income of the state, it would favour man's exercise of freedom, and so on. Some members of the Christian Democratic Party apparently went along with these views. After the case had been skillfully presented, a well-known Socialist stood up and delivered the shortest address ever recorded in Parliament: "And lead us not into temptation."

We cannot yearn for salvation for ourselves if we build a world that leads to temptation or one designed to function with structures and laws at best questionable; all this becomes institutionalized temptation against hope. Although we can never dispose of the messianic peace as if it were our own achievement, we can nevertheless make an investment in kindness, justice, truthfulness and thus promote peace on earth and render testimony to the power of the messianic peace.

If we ourselves are firmly grounded in hope, we shall work patiently and persistently for hope-inspiring conditions of life for others. We cannot comfort people with the hope of eternal life if we remain insensitive or cold to the hungry and the blind, if we are apathetic and unwilling to work for the improvement of the inhumane conditions of many jails and reformatories. There are wonderful families in Italy and in the United States who, during the past few years, have obtained permission for youths from local jails to live with their family. I know of one family of seven children that adopted a youngster who had already been tried several times; they extricated him from absolutely inhumane living conditions. He had been arrested for petty thievery; in jail he was repeatedly molested and raped by homosexuals. With the help of this loving family, he has turned into a very promising young man. Had he remained in jail, he would have been thoroughly perverted. I also know of a Protestant minister in the United States who has adopted a young Negro who had been repeatedly sent to jail; I was very impressed by the young man when I met him. He will, very likely, become a prominent leader in the black community; he is now living in a normal situation.

Shalom is above all the experience of an undeserved gift of God's bounty and therefore invites gratitude. But since it is a gift of the one Redeemer for the whole world, it includes an abundance of hope and love. Gratitude will therefore find expression in an unwavering commitment to reconciliation. The task of the whole priestly people of God and particularly of the ministerial priesthood can be viewed in this perspective of reconciliation.

Christ is the high priest who, in His blood, reconciles mankind with God and brings further reconciliation on earth. Those who receive the first fruits of redemption are enlisted in this service of reconciliation. "What I mean is, that God was in Christ reconciling the world to Himself, no longer holding men's misdeeds against them, and that He has entrusted us with the message of reconciliation. We come therefore as Christ's ambassadors. It is as if God were appealing to you through us: in Christ's name, we implore you, be reconciled to God!" (II Cor 5:19-20). With these words Paul speaks of his apostolic service but he also appeals to all the faithful to follow Christ who, for our sake, made Himself one with the sinfulness of man so that in Him we might be one with the goodness of God Himself and build up solidarity in peace.

Paul appeals to the community of Corinth in these terms: "Sharing in God's work, we urge this appeal upon you: you have received the grace of God; do not let it go for nothing" (II Cor 6:1). Paul had to cause tensions with the Judaeo-Christians in order to open the ministry of reconciliation to all men. But he is most careful not to create unnecessary tensions and hurts. "In order that our service may not be brought into discredit, we avoid giving offence in anything" (II Cor 6:3). In restating the meaning of the ministerial priesthood for this age, opening up new avenues for the future and unavoidably kindling new tensions, we have to see the organic unity between reconciliation with God and reconciliation in the world.

The priest, minister of reconciliation, has to be spiritually and psychologically prepared for the role of peacemaker without yielding to the temptation of seeking an easy peace. He must be able to maintain himself in the peace of Christ regardless of the pressures bearing upon him and to communicate this peace to others. In the midst of all the historically new events, he has

I

to let others know of the totally new event and hope, namely, the messianic peace, reconciliation with God and the hope for final brotherhood. He is to be a minister of peace and unity not only in spite of tensions but in the midst of tensions. The Acts of the Apostles tells us that the early apostolic community was one heart and one mind; yet, it does not conceal the growing-pains, the many tensions and crises through which the dynamics of the messianic peace were still manifest.

Christian hope never accepts a foul peace; only the false prophets cry out: "Peace! Peace!" where there is crying injustice and lack of sincerity. One needs the courage of the prophets to unmask false peace in order to make way for that peace which comes from God. Christ, the Prince of Peace, is the personification of saving conflict and mediating reconciliation. The ministerial priesthood should serve as exemplar for the whole priestly people of God that they may understand and accept their calling to be ambassadors of true peace. The life of today's priests should particularly proclaim what Paul communicates to the Corinthians in their tensions and dissensions: "Praise be to the God and Father of our Lord Jesus Christ, the all-merciful Father, the God whose consolation never fails us! He comforts us in all our troubles, so that we in turn may be able to comfort others in any trouble of theirs and to share with them the consolation we ourselves receive from God. As Christ's cup of suffering overflows, and we suffer with Him, so also through Christ our consolation overflows" (II Cor 1:3-5).

Even within the Church, reconciliation is never a *fait accompli* but a task always to be done anew. For the reconciliation of the different trends and currents, it would seem most important to focus on their complementarity. The ongoing reconciliation within the Church should be an example for reconciliation in the world. There can be peace and reconciliation only in a growing respect for pluralism, learning the art of dialogue and accepting, where need be, an open-ended compromise. Are we always aware that we cannot be a source of reconciliation for others unless we personally open ourselves in humble prayer and meditation for the undeserved peace and reconciliation? Only the prayerful man can be a minister of peace.

The messianic peace lies neither in bare horizontalism nor in an abstract verticalism. It is never at home where man seeks only consolation for his own soul nor does it come through those persons who are convinced that by themselves they can build a better world. The messianic peace is more than a social or cultural revolution; it never identifies itself with any specific culture or race. Only a humble Church that serves as a bond of unity for all the different trends, schools and cultures can have a good influence on the secular world.

From the perspective of "political theology", we can compare those trends of the Roman curia that would like to submit theology and the liturgy to the Latin "super-culture" with the temptation of the German race that led them to say in past decades: *"Am deutschen Wesen soll die Welt genesen"*, imposing the Germanic culture as a basis for the measurement of all others. Likewise, there are trends in the United States that claim the right of "messianic calling" for the American nation to be the "leader" and to tell all the other nations, for instance, to adopt their birth control programmes. The Church should be a witness that faith in Christ and the peace He imparts to us liberate man from all such claims and domineering attitudes.

While we stated emphatically that the messianic peace is more than a social gospel, the point must also be made that those who are truly ambassadors of reconciliation with God never fail to work for justice and peace. Yet, the Gospel is never tied up with any economic or political system; it remains always a healthy criticism, an appeal to reform. It never allows one to settle down with the *status quo*. The messianic peace not only calls for a continuous conversion but it also impels believers to commit themselves to development on all levels. Pope Paul VI has repeatedly expressed the same message in his own way: "Development is a new name for peace."

We celebrate the messianic peace in manifold ways but particularly in the sacrament of penance. We realize more than ever today that the sacrament of reconciliation is not a saving event tied up with a confessional box. The meaningful celebration of the sacrament of penance opens on all the horizons of peace, reconciliation and nonviolent action. Christians should some-

131

times be shamed and humbled by the commitment of humanists and men like Mahatma Gandhi to peace and nonviolence. Only if Christians absolutely commit themselves to peace can the world realize that Christ alone is peace and that religion is in no way an alienation. The disciples of Christ should be in the vanguard of any peace action; this will be the case if they are true believers.

Believers will not succumb to the illusion that they can construct an earthly paradise. They have the fortitude to face reality, to stand courageously in the midst of tension and to unmask all the idols endangering peace. We should not be unaware of the fact that a rejection of the hope of everlasting life is one of the sources of violence. If this world is our last hope, then it is easy to understand why men should want to kill each other for this last hope. But if peace in Christ and the promise of a final reconciliation sustain our hope, then we shall be ready to work patiently and at the cost of personal sacrifice for the reconciliation of the world. Our peace efforts cannot be based on some utopian messianism as was the case with a number of those who represented a "social gospel". If our common commitment to peace is commanded by the desire for reconciliation, it will be more realistic and more humble. Only if we put all our trust in Christ shall we display the necessary endurance and be able to give credit and trust to each other in an ongoing and occasionally demanding process of reconciliation.

The revealed truth that "love hopes everything" applies especially in relation to the daily experiences of human love: the hope to be loved, a love that hopes the loved one will fully find his true self. The expressed hope can awaken an astonishing response in the one who is honoured by such trust. If a parent or educator gives credit to a child or an adolescent, sincere efforts on the latter's part will reward the parent's trust. If you expect nothing good from a child, he will deteriorate. The same principle holds true for religious communities. There are cases of superiors who consistently and constantly need to prove that they are right in their opposition to a certain brother or sister. If failure comes, they triumphantly cry out: "I always said so." Little do they realize that the failure came mainly from the fact that they always thought and said so. They aborted hope by their lack of encouragement. The same pedagogical principle could apply to the faithful with respect to their bishop; if they give him credit they will often be astounded by how he manages his difficult task and can be truly a minister of unity and reconciliation. Those in authority who manifest a great trust in the work of God's grace and therefore in the good-will of those entrusted to their ministry will experience God's blessing. But those who disseminate suspicion and institutionalize distrust will reap the harvest.

The Apostle of the Gentiles himself missed this point in one instance while his friend Barnabas realized it better. Paul had certainly failed to give Mark credit when the latter had expected it. So Mark left him on the first great missionary journey after the first trying experiences of stoning and imprisonment; today, we would say: Mark took leave of absence. He later returned with Barnabas, driven by zeal and probably also by a great admiration for Paul. Paul did not reinstate him, but later on he did not try to prove that he himself was right. In his Epistle to the Colossians, he comments that of all the people of the circumcision, nobody works so well for the Gospel as Mark (Col 4:11). To Timothy, he writes to bring back Mark with him because he needs his help (II Tim 4:11). That Mark developed into a great missionary is due to the encouragement of Barnabas, who gave him credit when Paul did not; later Paul did give credit to Mark and he deserved it. This is the kind of human experience that is rooted in faith, in God's grace; it is conducive to a better and more vital appreciation of what trust in God means. In my opinion, such a human experience holds a "sacramental grace" because it is by God's creative and redemptive presence that we can perceive the connection between human trust and hope that comes from God and leads to him. A hope of eternal life that is incarnate is tremendously relevant; it includes temporal hope, mutual trust and encouragement inspired by ever greater hope. The peace of Christ can and will be the greatest force on earth if His disciples only make visible the fact that it bears fruit for the life of the world on all levels and on every occasion.

Chapter 14

THE ESCHATOLOGICAL VIRTUES

Central to every form of Christian witness are faith, love and the eschatological virtues. It is through Greek influence that the four cardinal virtues gained prominence in our moral teaching and set the direction of ascetical life. The fundamental thrust of the Bible does not come from prudence, self-control, fortitude and justice; the Bible is oriented towards hope. The Eucharist reminds us anew of the fundamental outlook of the Christian: hope in thanksgiving and hope in vigilance for present opportunities, for the coming of the Lord here-and-now and for His final coming.

Hope serves as the hub of the wheel of Christian virtues. Faith and love need to be permeated with hope because of the pilgrim situation in which the disciples of Christ find themselves. The Christian knows that he cannot attain final fulfilment on earth but he knows equally well how decisive this earthly life is with respect to final fulfilment. Hope is the indispensable dynamic force of faith and love. [1] Christian hope is based on loving *gratitude* for God's magnificent gifts and deeds. Without constant thanksgiving and praise, there is no freedom from anguish, bitterness and anger, no way of giving salvific and healing meaning to the many unavoidable frustrations.

---

[1] See Chapter 6: The Dynamism of Hope: Faith Active in Love.

135

It has been a very heartening experience for me to meet so many sisters and priests from different "houses of prayer". Among these religious and clergy there is a prevailing spirit of praise and gratitude; there is no room for bitterness and angry polarizations in these groups. It is not that these priests and sisters have become uncritical but their discernment is based on gratitude, appreciation and trust.

Gratitude is a function of the Christian outlook of hope; one imbued with hope renders thanks always and everywhere. The model is Christ Himself who, on the way to Calvary, gives thanks to His Father for having sent Him in poverty to be the obedient Servant in the great design of the salvation of mankind. The distinctive characteristic of the Christian shaped by the Eucharist is his ability to render thanks for all things in all situations; he can sing the Canticle of the Sun, he can praise God even for Brother Death and his human frailty.

In a parish where I had been preaching, I was surprised to find a great spirit of faith and such responsiveness on the part of the people to the point that I queried the pastor. "Can you tell me what you have done to bring about such openness? How do you account for it? I have noticed a unique spirit of faith, of trust and zeal." He replied at once: "Neither I nor my curate is responsible, though he is a good man. You must go and see a certain spinster who has renewed the parish." I accepted the suggestion and paid her a visit; she had been bed-ridden for over twenty years. Even with great effort, she could not move her arms and hands sufficiently to feed herself. She was totally dependent on others for all personal care. However she was radiantly at peace and her peace of mind was a source of inspiration, trust and faith for the whole parish. I asked her to explain to me the source of her joy. "When this illness struck me, I made a pilgrimage to Lourdes expecting a miraculous cure, but when I saw all the suffering, I asked God to let me offer this affliction for the salvation of the world. Since then, I have come to understand better what a joy it is to be able to offer something of myself with Christ for the salvation of mankind." The tiny room of that virgin lady was the centre of the whole parish; it radiated a spirit of faith and gratitude even amid great suffering. She could live joyfully because she was so fully united with Christ.

The true Christian gratefully accepts whatever happens to him in any given situation. During November of last year, death claimed one of my dearest friends, a confrère 93 years old; he had earlier asked me to give him extreme unction when he felt his last hour had come. I complied and spent the night with him. About three hours after receiving the sacrament, he recovered his voice and asked: "Tell me, what is the name of the author who wrote that magnificent book, *Ita, Pater*?" I told him: Father Graeff. "Now is the moment for my last 'Yes, Father'." I then asked him how he felt. "I am very happy; I am so happy . . ." and these were his last words. This elderly man had truly accepted the spirit of Vatican II and all the ensuing changes as something he had always hoped for all his life.

The Christian spirit of gratitude is one that can accept change; it is a gratitude rooted in the Paschal Mystery where selfishness is put to death, where the horizon is open, where man has gained his freedom to serve the whole people of God in Christ. The Eucharist connotes the full dimension of this gratitude in hope. When the Christian looks back he does not do so with a sour face like the wife of Lot; he looks back in thankfulness marvelling at the wonderful deeds of God. His thanksgiving for daily events is staked on the manifestation of God's love, in the passion, death and resurrection of the Lord. Thus, with a gratitude based on God's fidelity, on everything he has done, the Christian can look back knowing that God, who has so wonderfully begun His work in creation is pursuing it in an ineffable way in Jesus Christ and will fulfil it in Him on the day of the parousia. So it is a celebration of hope in thanksgiving and a celebration of gratitude in hope.

By looking back on the great deeds of God and waiting for the final fulfilment, the Christian is not alienating himself from the reality of life. He is always ready to fathom the full import of the present moment because he knows that here and now he is meeting Christ in his brothers and sisters and in all of God's children. The Christian loves the whole world with

J

Christ's love; he discovers the mark of salvation in human history. So his thanksgiving and hope will not allow him to be alienated or estranged from life. Rather, they commit him in a redeeming way to the world which yearns for a share in the freedom gained by gratitude and liberating hope.

Gratitude and hope yield *vigilance for the kairos;* it is an essential and basic principle of Christian ethics to be alert for the present opportunities. "The hymn says: 'Sleeper awake; rise from the dead and Christ will shine upon you.' Use to the fullest the present opportunity" (Eph 5:14-16). If we are awake, if we gratefully grasp the full import of God's work and words and if we view all events with hope and as leading towards final fulfilment, then it is impossible to live the present moment superficially and distractedly; it must be lived with the light of Christ shining upon us. We can then perceive the wealth and depth of the here and now, the real opportunities to serve our brethren and to praise God in our daily work and encounters.

The Christian does not live in an "if and but" world but with a daily "Yes, Father, here I am" to the Lord's calling. He accepts the limited possibilities and patiently bears the heat of the day; he can equally well adjust to the chilly weather and the depressing moments of life, exhibiting a trust that transcends the painful moment. As human beings and sons of Adam, we always have a certain propensity to escape and become alienated from reality, but when we are led by the Spirit of Christ we are set free for the real task. Through the gifts of the Holy Spirit, we can recognize all the gifts God has given us as an appeal, a gracious invitation to serve our brethren. The liturgy helps us to see things in a broader light and helps to place in perspective daily realities; it teaches us the great art of being realistic and truly sets us on the path with the Lord. We are not encapsulated forever in the present moment; this would be an establishment, the end of all hope. We look forward, living in the present tense while keeping an eye on the future.

Another eschatological virtue fundamentally rooted in the Bible is *readiness to change,* the willingness to learn and unlearn in fidelity to the Lord of history. It refers to our common prerogative which bears the stamp of God's guarantee: the privilege to err or to make mistakes. This should motivate us to cultivate the most important attitude in this respect, namely, the courage to make mistakes. I have a very gifted friend who can read and understand a number of foreign languages but he has never learned to speak a second language because of his fear of mistakes. We learn very little if we do not risk making mistakes. Parents who do not allow their teenagers or children ever to make mistakes are merely educating them for infantilism. All of us have the right and privilege to err, but this does not mean that we must indulge in calculated mistakes. In our effort to do what is right we must run the risk of being mistaken occasionally; it is all part of the learning process. It is equally the privilege of the Roman Catholic Church to err because she is a pilgrim Church. We should not be so niggardly as to deprive bishops and the dear Holy Father himself of their good right to err occasionally.

In the fourteenth century, Pope John XXII taught that the separated souls would not see God before the parousia. It was a great mistake for which he was blamed and immediately censored by theologians; he did not complicate the issue but apologized. In his testament he stated that if he had erred, he felt sure God would forgive him because he had made the mistake through simple ignorance and not out of arrogance. This is true Christian humility, an attitude that could ultimately make the institution of the papacy acceptable to our separated brethren. If all Christians and all Churches adopted a humble attitude, it would greatly help eliminate bitterness. We have a serious problem posed today by the millions of self-styled "infallible popes", people who criticize violently and are very intolerant because they are not aware of their own limitations. If we all enjoy the privilege of making mistakes, we also have the corresponding duty to acknowledge our mistakes and correct them.

Readiness to change arises from and leads to fidelity if it is in harmony with the perspective indicated by the Paschal Mystery which we commemorate and celebrate in the Eucharist. Change should not be merely for the sake of change nor for making detours, but change should be based on our longing to find the best entrance to the Lord's highways. Consequently, our changes should be the result of meditation, prayer, and painstaking effort to know the real situation, the alternatives offered to us in the here-and-now in order to find the most appropriate step leading towards final fulfilment. It means a readiness to change in fidelity to the Lord of history; as creative fidelity, it necessarily entails the courage of risk in humility. No doubt exists that those who vigorously promote ecumenism are taking risks in view of the hope for unifying all Christians. Mistakes are made and will be made in this effort, but infinitely greater is the risk of settling for lifelessness and separateness forever. If the Church dare not take risks, she will be, at worst, a graveyard, and at best, a rundown refuge for old people. We can take the risk of life only with prayer, humility and that courage which arises from trust in God. Life and risks are possible only if we finally entrust ourselves to the Lord of history, trusting fully that he is guiding us and healing us.

Epikeia represents the courage to take risks in the realm of traditional teaching. Those who exhibit this virtue know well that it would be a vicious attitude to cling to the letter of the law for security's sake when it is against the great law of love in responsibility. St. Thomas Aquinas finds that the adult Christian striving towards maturity is duty-bound to prefer a possible error by seeking the spirit of the law to the committing of a very probable error against the law of love by clinging to the letter of the law. If we rigidly abide by the letter of the law without attempting to search for its deeper spirit, we have not yet reached even the minimal level of morality. I find it a sign of hope that so many Christians today are yearning for a more profound understanding of the Lord's great commandment of love and its articulation in daily life; they thereby indicate willingness to assume risks with new ventures. However, we must not take risks about important matters without prayer and without examining our conscience and motives, asking ourselves whether or not we have done our best (not the impossible) to know the full situation. We must learn to discern in the light of the full scale and urgency of human values.

Another eschatological virtue, therefore, is *discernment* with respect to complex present-day historical situations. Discernment presupposes a constant readiness to learn what constitute the proper criteria for carrying on a dialogue with others while being respectfully docile to the magisterium. Discernment must always be exercised in solidarity with a view to building up the Mystical Body; it calls for a distinction between what is in accord with the law of growth and the total vocation of man and how best under the present circumstances to serve God and to witness to Him, the Lord of history, while remaining sensitive to the needs of people.

A distinctly eschatological virtue which seems to have been rediscovered in our own day is that of *nonviolence* which may be defined as the patient and firm action on behalf of a more just and humane world without ever resorting to inhumane means. This is one of the most important virtues or attitudes contributing to renewal of the Church and helping promote a genuinely Christian "revolution" in the world that looks forward to more humane conditions.

Karl Marx was convinced that only by feeding class hatred and increasing tension, by preparing for a final explosion of violence, would mankind attain perfect harmony, peace, brotherhood and unselfishness for which the proletariat longed. His theories were a strange mixture of so-called science and apocalyptic prophecy. The Christian hopes for a world of justice and peace, that is, a humane world and one of brotherhood beyond this world, but this very hope determines the goal and means of his commitment. He is committed to working for a nonviolent revolution in the spirit of the Gospel. When the disciples of Christ try to be good, kind and merciful to each other like God who revealed His goodness and mercy in Jesus Christ, we witness a very radical kind of transformation indeed. A Gospel-based revolution seeks that kind of action, those structures and publicly shared convictions that promote nonviolence on all sides.

We are committed to the world because of our hope for peace in Christ. We believe that the messianic peace has already

141

appeared to us in Christ and that Christ leads us to His own nonviolent actions, the highest form of activity, towards a total commitment to peace on earth.

There are great hopes but also serious threats to progress in nonviolent attitudes and action in our day. Gandhi was certainly a man who, in a quite extraordinary way, embodied nonviolence, co-operation for peace and justice, and absolute respect for the human dignity of all men; his inspirations flowed from his firm hope. He laid down the following conditions for nonviolent action: a deep union with God (therefore, at the very outset of his career, he founded an *ashram,* a house of prayer) and a constructive plan (nonviolence was never to be understood as a mere tactic; it had to be a spirituality, an abiding attitude of respect and love). Nonviolent protest and action do honour to those against whom they are directed; the protest informs them that they have not been written off as unimportant. Gandhi believed that we must never give up hope that those who today oppress and oppose us will some day be our friends. He achieved this goal with eventual friendship between the Indian and the British peoples. This is certainly one of the greatest achievements of this century.

Martin Luther King is another example of nonviolence who still has many followers; our hopes and the times call for still more followers. In Brazil Archbishop Helder Camara is one of the great forces for justice and united nonviolent action. He is right in warning that violence will of necessity increase unless a common effort is made on all sides vigorously to promote justice by all nonviolent means. Inaction on one side and the oppressive use of power on the other will result in violent explosions without truly freeing man. Bishop Camara is as convinced as was Gandhi of the necessity of that kind of prayer life which is the source of hope nourishing the spirit of nonviolence in action. A house of prayer intended to be a school of prayer and nonviolence is now being set up in Recife.

Nonviolence belongs to one of the seven words or injunctions of the Lord: "But I tell you . . ." and it can be the greatest force, a great strength but only if it is rooted in unlimited hope. When hope is fading away, nonviolent action becomes a mere technique and can explode in new forms of violence or the hypocritical use of seemingly nonviolent tactics in a violent spirit.

Nonviolence is more than a technique that can be learned. However, there are aspects that can be mastered; there must be a place for the charisms of intuition, imagination and design, but the source of strength remains hope. The basis lies in that deep union with God, trusting that those who walk with God in peace can be peacemakers. However, it also entails a willingness to pay the cost of discipleship; this spells the real difference between a Christian understading of nonviolence and nonviolence as a bare political technique or tactic.

Chapter 15

ACTING ON THE WORD

Towards the end of the Gospel of St. John, there is a startling story about a little misunderstanding which helps us appreciate more the deeper meaning of Christian life. Once Peter had been reconciled by the Lake of Tiberias, reassured in his friendship with the Lord and confirmed in his ministry of unity, he "looked around and saw the disciple whom Jesus loved following — the one who at supper had leaned back close to Him to ask the question, 'Lord, who is it that will betray you?' When he caught sight of him, Peter asked, 'Lord, what will happen to him?' " (Jn 21:20-22). Peter seems to feel that John was more deserving of the ministry of unity than he was because he had stood the test of loyalty far better. Peter has obviously lost his excessive trust in himself; it is no longer the Peter of "Everyone else may fall away but I will not" (Mk 14:29). Peter had experienced the power of the Lord's mercy, of the Lord's Passion and now asks: "what will become of him?" Jesus answers: "If it should be my will that he wait until I come, what is it to you? Follow me."

"That saying of Jesus became current in the brotherhood, and was taken to mean that that disciple would not die. But in fact, Jesus did not say that he would not die; he only said: 'If it should be my will that he wait until I come, what is it to you?' It is this same disciple who attests what has been written here" (Jn 21:22-24). John, with the penetrating eye of the eagle, recognizes the Lord when he comes under any disguise; he is the witness of the Gospel and to the Gospel of hope. The Lord did not say that John would not die before the parousia: he did something more. He revealed the character and charism of John to be one of constantly waiting for the coming of the Lord in all events, with Christ-like vigilance and love for his neighbours and the needs of the community.

The whole Church could be transformed if this episode were properly understood. It is said to Peter: "what is it to you?" Peter cannot understand his ministry as Supreme Head without John, that is, without that other ministry or charism of John that should characterize the whole Church even in her institutional aspect: waiting for the coming of the Lord. An enlightening parallelism could be drawn comparing this episode in the Gospel of St. John with chapters 3, 5 and 6 of the conciliar document of the Church, *Lumen Gentium,* which deal with the ministry of the pope and the bishops and the *charisma* of those totally dedicated to the kingdom of God through the charism of the evangelical counsels.

The eschatological virtues mentioned in the preceding chapter are particularly indispensable for persons called to live according to the evangelical counsels. Celibacy for the heavenly kingdom and the evangelical witness to poverty can be lived only by those who behold the great vision of gratitude, hope and docility to the Holy Spirit. The counsels entail vigilance with respect to the here and now, a readiness to change direction in response to the fidelity of the living God of history, and the courage to take risks. Everything flows from the evangelical spirit of *poverty,* the gift of the Holy Spirit who renews hearts and the face of the earth. Poverty must be understood in the light of that great witness to heaven, Christ, who was in His divinity the Word of God but who, in the greatest miracle of freedom, makes Himself a servant. He obediently fulfils the great design of the Father to manifest the full extent and depth of His love (Phil 2: 6-8). Rich as He was, He made Himself poor in order to enrich all of us by His poverty. Christ made Himself the Servant Messiah so as to express His fullness and the plenitude of His love, emptying Himself of everything but love and loving us even to death on the cross. The spirit of poverty receives its strongest testimony in the very last words of Jesus: "Father, into Your hands I commit My spirit."

Those who dedicate themselves to a life according to the evangelical counsels commit themselves above all to a continuous conversion, a constant openness to the Spirit and a readiness to empty themselves of whatever impinges on their liberty or their freedom to serve and to love unselfishly. The highest values cannot be possessed by power; they are the free gifts of God bestowed upon those who open themselves humbly and gratefully to them.

Everyday experience proves that if we want to love a person truly, we must above all respect that person's freedom. If we try to force a person to love us or want to possess that person, we can never elicit the free response that is love; love is a response in freedom. So poverty must permeate our whole lives whether it be in marriage or in religious life. Poverty means freedom to serve, the freedom to sense the needs of others, a freedom which respects and guarantees the freedom of other persons, assuring them that they will never be instrumentalized or devoured.

Evangelical poverty is not a discrete entity apart from hope and love; it is the initial manifestation of joy, the wealth of a person who knows that he is truly loved by the greatest Lover, Christ. It is the realization that all things, especially our capacities, are marvellous gifts, a tremendous wealth, because they are more than mere possessions. They are signs of God's own love and signs of His goodness, and thus promises and signs of hope. Therefore, any person who, with all that he is and all that he has, places himself at the service of his brethren, the service of the common good, is a "sacrament", a remarkable sign and witness of eschatological hope. Such a person shows gratitude for things already begun, proclaims the wealth of love already manifest, and hopes for the plenitude of love yet unseen but guaranteed by God. This helps him to make the best possible use of present opportunities and possibilities for action, even very modest and insignificant occasions.

Christ Himself is the witness to heaven, the witness to hope because of His *obedience*. His is not a slavish obedience however, but an expression of the highest degree of freedom; He freely binds Himself to His brethren agreeing to be their servant and Redeemer. It is one of the noblest manifestations of man's freedom to be able to bind himself to fidelity by conjugal vows, religious vows or any other great, irrevocable commitment. Such an act is a tremendous exercise of freedom but one that needs revitalization every day. Such a commitment cannot be assured once and for all by a "yes" at the altar on the wedding day; the spouses have to learn and constantly relearn the meaning of genuine love. When illusions have collapsed and the very core of the other person becomes exposed, then is the time to realize that one's earlier "yes" freely uttered really commits one to further growth in freedom now, growth in depth and in courage. The situation is very similar in the case of religious vows; like Moses setting out and looking forward, the religious will find new horizons opening up, but the true religious will accept the daily insecurities because of his firm trust in God, which gives him a sense of security that has nothing in common with the security complex of those who are always seeking themselves.

Obedience opens our eyes to the needs of the community. One who commits himself to obedience becomes the freest servant imaginable since he intends only to serve, to guarantee the dignity of each person in the community and to promote the unity and solidarity of all. Mature obedience inspires hope in the person who is fully committed to the common good. Disobedience can be a fault in leaders as well as in non-leaders; the difference is only one of degree although it might express itself in a variety of ways. For instance, those leaders or religious superiors who will not allow persons gifted with charisms such as good ideas, imagination, a sense of humour, or the ability to criticize constructively, to place their talents, their wealth, at the service of the common good, are truly disobedient. Leaders must be eminently obedient to the common good and welfare of the group; they must stand ready always to examine their motives in the form of service expected of them. In certain cases it may be that the highest form of obedience in service to the common good is to retire; this could well represent the superior's or bishop's last great contribution to the community. Today, religious are in general a sign of hope; most congregations have by now eliminated their "eternal fathers" and "eternal mothers". Such courage should inspire the Church to free herself from "eternal bishops".

It is a great sign of vigilance and obedience to the common good when a bishop resigns at the proper moment. The question asked of young men being ordained to the priesthood: "Do you promise obedience?" should be understood as: "Do you promise obedience to the common good?" This includes obedience to the legitimate bearer of authority who, in turn, must be able to obey and to submit himself in all things to the dictates of the common good.

Many religious orders and congregations have paved the way. They elect their superior general or general minister for six years after which he becomes Father Cooke or Father Schmidt like any other; this is freedom in service. After serving the community for six years as a major superior, he is freed to serve it in the most humble and loving way and the community, in turn, is free to look for the best new servant of unity and servant of the common good. Closely related to this power of freedom is the concept of *collegiality* which liberates those in the service of unity from all forms of isolation, allowing them to share each other's experiences, to exchange reflections and insights systematically, and thus to know and be in a better position to serve the community. Such a sharing of experiences is authentic obedience because it fosters a genuine freedom to serve the common good.

One of my first sessions in the confessional brought me a precious experience of how to understand obedience. A male penitent came to me and said: "I was disobedient to my wife." I told him candidly that I was quite inexperienced as a confessor, that I was learning and needed his help. . "We were always told that the wife is to obey the husband. Why do you confess that you disobeyed your wife?" — "Oh, Father, it was quite clear: she was right!" I must add that my gentleman was a little uneasy when I asked him: "Would you accept as penance

149

telling your wife that she was right?" History abounds with stories illustrating the point that it is difficult for those bound by certain traditions and structures to recognize that others are right. A pope, a bishop or a religious superior is truly free and serves freely the people under him if he does not think only of his own superiority but recognizes genuine authority in those who can point convincingly to the best way of serving the common good. We have then a display of evangelical obedience in the exercise of authority.

Whenever I refer to the witness of *chastity*, I intend to include premarital and conjugal chastity, the chastity of the widow and of divorced persons, and the consecrated chastity of those who dedicate themselves to the Gospel or to the service of the needy. Chastity confers great freedom. If we thirst and hunger for God's rightful rule to prevail, if we appreciate union with God as the highest good, if we respect the person of others and revere them as children of God, then chastity becomes for us a source of hope and harvest of hope. Chastity strengthens hope just as hope strengthens chastity. I am not referring to any kind of reward for oneself for having renounced the joys of the world; I do not consider sour old maids or cantankerous bachelors as "virgins". I consider eminently chaste those who are able to love without consuming or possessing the other person, who can love in freedom and also receive love in absolute freedom. Celibacy for the sake of the kingdom means a completely radical decision never to possess another person.

In Christian marriage the mystery emerges also when the marriage has truly become a sign of union and hope. The great Protestant theologian, Karl Barth, considers it a serious duty of the Christian minister to alert young people to the two great possibilities of choice before them: they can either serve God in celibacy for His kingdom or serve Him in marriage. He is convinced that if we no longer have the witness of those who have embraced celibacy for the heavenly kingdom in great freedom, then many people will feel "condemned to marriage". Single women and bachelors would then become the "left-overs" of marriage choices. Barth's statement strongly supports the witness of religious men and women for freedom. It is because of the joy of the Gospel and that deep realization that God has given the celibate so many signs of love that he does not feel bound to one way of life, namely, that of serving God in marriage, albeit a very great and meritorious way. Marriage is also a calling to holiness, but unless there is freedom inspired by trust in God and hope in everlasting life, neither marriage nor celibacy can be considered a vocation because the latter presupposes the free choice of a state of life. Both must witness to that hope which stems from gratitude for all that God has given us. In marriage we rightly expect to encounter chastity that preserves the freedom of the other person and never consumes or uses the other person as an object.

In some circles, there is much sensless talk about self-fulfilment; there are claims made that one cannot fulfil oneself unless one has an exclusive friend or companion of the opposite sex. This is tantamount to devouring the other person and leads unavoidably to mutual frustration. Genuine friendship is characterized by reverence and is respectful of the other person's life and calling.

The life of one of the greatest German theologians, Johann Adam Möhler was a marvellous witness to this kind of freedom. His famous book on the Church already breathed the spirit of Vatican II more than a century ago. Möhler was a seminarian, and during his last long vacation before becoming a subdeacon, he met a wonderful young lady with whom he fell in love. They came to a mutual confession of love for each other. In all sincerity, the young girl asked him if he had been sure of his calling to the priesthood before meeting her. The young man replied as sincerely: "Yes, I was sure." She then admitted: "I will never possess you against your true vocation." This noble gesture helped him see his celibate priestly vocation in a new light, as freedom to renounce a selfish desire, trusting that what God wanted was greater than a beautiful human dream.

Those who truly live the evangelical counsels, therefore, constitute a sign of hope for the world; their way of life manifests the great freedom to love in the way of Christ. Christ did not come to build a home for His own family but to dedicate Himself to the whole family of God. However, religious life must be seen in an absolute unifying perspective with the witness of Christian spouses who are searching for the will of God in all things. They are companions on pilgrimage towards eternal life; they communicate to their children through unselfish love the gladdening news of God who is in their midst as their redeeming partner and companion on the path preparing for eternal life.

The present period of turmoil, transition and renewal signals the need of the Church for the great witness of fidelity and hope provided by religious men and women who unceasingly strive to be credible signs of the liberating power, joy and love which enable all to answer their own calling and to serve with the fullness of their personality. If we believe in the resurrection of the Lord, namely, that death in Christ is the highest expression of freedom preparing us for the great revelation of the resurrection, then it makes sense to live according to the evangelical counsels and to be a witnessing sign for the pilgrim Church, singing hymns and songs, and rendering thanks to God.

In this light, I feel that a life fully in accord with the evangelical counsels can be a hopeful "yes" to God's word, to God's work and to His world, because it is directed towards the final fulfilment which is the fullest freedom and the all-embracing power of unselfish love. A life based on the evangelical counsels can help to restore that freedom which God originally planned and which Christ came to restore. It can manifest the beginning of the final fulfilment. It can be a forceful "yes" to life and to that freedom guaranteed by Christ.

How blessed are those who come to that freedom in which they wholeheartedly adore not only by words but by their whole being the absolute freedom of God to guide and transfigure us. Man reaches his greatest hope on earth when he removes all obstacles to God's gracious action.

Chapter 16

HOPE FOR THE "HOPELESS"

When I hear pastors and superiors speaking about "hopeless cases", I cannot help but reflect: where is their faith in God? Where is their hope? According to the optimistic outlook of the Gospel, there is truly no hopeless case, no hopeless situation; God calls everybody to forgiveness and repentance.

I am thinking especially of the situation of homosexuals, drug addicts, drunkards or people suffering from any kind of neurotic or other psychopathological weakness. Psychology has helped us come to a better understanding of their difficulties; we know that the attitude "you are a hopeless case" only helps to promote their feelings of inadequacy and misery. If we give them credit, if we respect them as persons and appreciate any positive step in the direction of change, they can respond with greater alacrity. Their efforts are highly valued by God, more so perhaps than our seemingly bigger steps, because God always looks to good-will.

With homosexuals, we must carefully distinguish voluntary perversion from a weakness which can be a source of great suffering. Some years ago I wrote a series of articles in an Italian periodical about the problems of *masturbation* and *homosexuality*. I insisted on how important it was to distinguish between sin and suffering. The afflicted person very often needs to be helped to accept the great suffering of sex deviancy; the painful experience is often intensified by an inability to distinguish be-

153

tween the extent of guilt and the degree of illness; such people must therefore be comforted for any display of good-will. When there is good-will, an initial effort and acceptance of suffering, there is a basis for hope, a sign of God's saving presence. I was cheered by the responses to my series including visits and letters. One correspondent wrote: "I was at the point of hanging myself as useless for this world. I am a poor homosexual; I now realize that even this dirty sickness can be a part of redemption and I am relieved. I know now that I am not a hopeless case." If we can get the afflicted person to look at the problem in this light, there is no reason to doubt that therapy would not be successful.

Many homosexuals can be helped and possibly cured if instead of passing judgment on them we differentiate between sin and suffering, between what can be eliminated and what must be accepted. More preventive and rehabilitative measures are needed; psychological help must be available to all who cannot obtain help from qualified educators, pastors and ministers. Appropriate motivation and more positive attitudes towards helping the psychologically impaired person will help make Christian morality more credible to modern man than the passing of harsh judgments and issuing of imperatives based on an inadequate knowledge of man and the world. The shocking problems of homosexuality, drug addiction and other psychopathological tendencies call for a more constructive approach based on a painstaking scientific study of the causes.

A few years ago, I conducted a workshop for Italian social workers. The group was organized by a sister of Father Lombardi, and Mrs. Merlin, a member of the famous Socialist Party; these social workers were totally dedicated to the rehabilitation of women abused in *prostitution*. During the entire workshop I did not once hear the word "prostitutes" mentioned; they were referred to as "friends" out of respect for the dignity of the person. They described their approach to these women in serious need of help. When their clients succeeded in limiting their sexual contacts to one man, the case worker expressed grateful delight over the first success. However, when expressing appreciation for this progress and thanking them for their effort, they made the client realize that it was a reassuring indication that she was now ready for the next step forward. They encouraged the women to progress further by telling them what they could be in time; they were given an understanding of their worth as persons and of their potential for a good marriage. These 70 social workers are continuing to do marvellous work because of their respect inspired totally by their faith in a God of mercy and Redeemer of all. No one is excluded in the Saviour's plan; he came to save all, and the redeeming action of Christ can be communicated better if we know the totality of a person's difficulties, her psychological make-up, the limited possibilities of her environment and the heritage and burden from the past. However, within this realm, miracles can happen, especially when there is evidence of hope and faith in those attempting to assist their weaker brethren.

When I was still teaching near Munich, I would from time to time hear the confession of a converted Magdalen. She had been persuaded to lead a better life by a reformed Magdalen who had become a great apostle. Once the dignity of these women has been rescued and they are confirmed in Christ's friendship, they approach other Magdalens bringing them the hope that is rooted in faith and gratitude. Even when they fall again and return for help, there must be praise to God who never abandons persons in need but gives them strength to start anew. Each effort and each contact is a sign that God wants to renew that person.

A very serious problem is posed by our present *judicial and penal system*. In spite of considerable progress, the courts still observe double standards; we have laws for the poor and others for the rich or influential. Minor transgressions of the law by the poor fill the court records while the rich man pays for an "off-the-record" settlement. Youths jailed for petty thievery or other minor offences usually become perverted and frustrated in jail. Our society should be less pharisaical. What is needed is a sounder pedagogical and rehabilitative approach that would enlist the co-responsibility of all the members of society and its institutions. It behoves concerned citizens to suggest and take steps to introduce legislation that will support the rehabilitative efforts of the social agencies. A trained worker coming from a rehabilitation centre is often refused employment because of a prison record and/or a history of drug addiction. In such cases, we have the legislative branch of the local or state government working at cross-purposes with the judicial and penal branch for which they appropriate money. The readiness with which we condemn transgressors of our social and juridical norms is too often associated with a comfortable "easy" conscience on the part of citizens. A more constructive approach would regard the social problems or evils of drug addiction, prostitution and homosexuality as an appeal to renew our sense of co-responsibility and to work for the reform of social structures.

The problem of *remarried persons who had been divorced* is under serious study today; there are a number of books and many articles on this topic. I refer to a few of my own articles, one of which was published in *The Jurist:* "Internum Forum Solutions for Insoluble Marriage Cases".[1] Such cases are "insoluble" but not hopeless; they may be without solution for canonists in view of the present system of canon law, but a law cannot be the last word for men of good-will; such people must be offered a solution of hope, good news for a sincere conscience. If a couple is living together in peace and a separation would harm either party or be a cause of hardship for others, we cannot advise them to leave one another. In most circumstances, they cannot convince themselves that they should try to live together in total continence (as brother and sister). The harmony of their life together and the peace of an upright conscience demand a solution in understanding.

Two years ago a Sicilian gentleman came to me together with his brother to discuss his marital problems. I indicated the possibility of moving to another room so as to be able to discuss the matter privately with him. But he objected saying that his brother knew of his plight; he wanted him to hear the discussion

---

[1] Bernard Häring, "Internum Forum Solutions for Insoluble Marriage Cases", *The Jurist,* (January, 1970), 21-30. See also my other article, "Pastoral Work Among the Divorced and Invalidly Married", *Concilium,* V (May, 1970), 123-130.

because he had been the only person to help him. In brief, the details of the situation were as follows: when he returned from the war he found that his young wife had had two children by another man. He offered to be reconciled and adopt the two children but she refused on both counts. His brother repeatedly acted as a go-between reiterating that all would be forgiven, but she declined his offer and never returned. Since his brother had many children he could not be accommodated in that home; so he lived alone, forcibly an isolated being. As time went on, he felt it would be better for him to remarry but this could not be in the Church. He now has eight children. His brother assured me that he had never missed Mass; he and his wife never forgot their evening prayer; they prayed the rosary together in spite of their being excluded from the sacraments. I gave him absolution, after which I contacted the bishop of that diocese and told him I had given absolution to the gentleman.

It is a scandal to exclude such good men from the sacramental life of the Church. However, since most people are not yet prepared to understand exceptional cases, I advised him to receive Communion where he was not known. As far as my experience goes, there is a growing consensus that we should educate people to mature discernment. Then nobody would cry "scandal" when these people receive Communion because nobody can doubt their good will. Whether or not these marriage problems can be properly regulated according to canon law is another matter. In many cases the first marriage was probably never a valid one. The present continuing revision of canon law should seek to facilitate matters for many people in the future. It is very obvious that my Sicilian gentleman could not be expected to leave the mother of his children. Together they have worked out their Communion as a sign of fidelity, trust and mutual care, and they are the messengers of faith and hope to their children.

Another problematic marriage situation came to my attention two years ago while I was on an East coast engagement addressing a large group of CCD teachers. A young man about 20 years old came to me and asked if I would have time to see his father; he did not feel he could carry on much longer. I immediately asked for details about his situation. He replied:

we are eight boys; when my mother died, I was 12 and the eldest. My father tried hard to find a mother for us but no Catholic woman wanted to inherit such a herd of boys. Every housekeeper left because things kept going from bad to worse. Finally, an Anglican lady, who had been divorced years earlier but who lived a good life, had compassion, married him and accepted us all; my brothers have received her well. She is the most marvellous person we could have hoped for. The Sunday following his marriage, my father was an usher in church; the pastor devoted his whole sermon to him, condemning him to the deepest hell. At home, we now have order and there is love in our family; only, my father is becoming more and more depressed." I told the young man to ask his father to come and see me. When he called, I could only say: "What more could I ask of you now?" As in the previous case, he had never missed Mass; he saw to the proper education of his children. His eldest son would not have been in CCD work if the father had not cared for them. This family also prayed together. I gave him absolution and told him not to show up in his parish as it was not a sign of hope for him. He could receive Communion somewhere else where there would be no loveless talk and no scandal.

The problem with which the Church is grappling today is whether a marriage which is *hopelessly* destroyed imposes life-long celibacy on the abandoned spouse. Where there is still a possibility of restoring it, we must imitate God's covenant with his people and regard it as irrevocable. He grants forgiveness whenever his people return to him, and he tirelessly calls men to repentance and promises forgiveness. Similarly as long as a marriage can be saved, it must be saved.

But if the marriage is thoroughly dissolved with no hope of reviving it, then the question is not so much whether we can tear asunder what God has put together as "was it ever put together by God in the first place?" In many instances, we have good reason to suspect that the marriage was not put together by God because of the gap between the spouses which could never possibly be bridged. Was this coloured girl in New York destined by God for this 17-year-old boy who got her pregnant when she was only 16? The mother forced the girl to marry him in church. The following night, he pulled out a knife and assaulted her; she still wears the scars from those deep wounds. After a few months she ran away frightened because of his repeated threats to her life. The ecclesiastical marriage court says: nothing can be done since the marriage was performed in church. There is at least a 99% probability that such a marriage was never ordained by God and only a very remote probability that it was; canonists should take this into consideration. Now this poor girl had a history of drug addiction. A group of nuns took the girl into their community in an effort to rehabilitate her but she will surely return to drugs if she cannot remarry. We have to look at the whole situation. Morality is for people; if our laws and the application of moral principles do not express a concern for people, they are not promoting the common good.

Tradition shows that the Oriental Churches which constituted the great part of Christendom in the first few centuries, have already appealed to *"oikonomia"*, that is, an application of moral principles and laws according to the "salvific distribution" of God's mercy. If it can be shown that the first marriage was hopelessly destroyed, if the abandoned spouse had no hope of a reconciliation and could not live as a celibate for the heavenly kingdom without suffering great harm, then they would tolerate a second marriage. Such a marriage was not accorded a celebration because it was not reason for rejoicing, but rather it was blessed in the form of a penitential service with the assurance of divine forgiveness. At times, the local churches expressed their reservations by excluding from the sacraments for a 30-day period the separated spouses who had remarried.

At the Council of Trent, a large number of bishops wanted to condemn explicitly this more merciful practice of the Oriental Churches but the representatives and bishops of the republic of Venice intervened. Venice controlled a number of dioceses in the Orient where Catholics and Orthodox lived side by side under the authority of a Latin bishop and they knew about the Orthodox tradition. After prolonged discussion it was decided that while condemning a Protestant position which asserted that adultery dissolves the marriage, the Council would defend the practice and doctrine of the Latin Church but would refrain from any overt condemnation of the ancient practice of the Orthodox Churches.

I want to state unambiguously that I adhere to the doctrine of Trent which teaches: "If one should say that the Church erred while she taught and still teaches according to the evangelical and apostolic doctrine (see Mk 10; I Cor 7): that the bond of marriage cannot be dissolved because of the adultery of the other spouse and that both, including the innocent spouse who has not given occasion to adultery, cannot remarry during the lifetime of the other spouse; that a man who divorces his adulterous wife and marries another or the wife who divorces the adulterous husband and marries another commits adultery — let him be anathema." [1] The editors of the *Enchiridion symbolorum* assert in a footnote to this text that the Greeks were not condemned by this statement since they did not oppose this doctrine of the Latin Church. Indeed, the doctrine is one that inspires hope and educates towards hope. Even in the case of adultery, the innocent party must not be obdurate; he must do his best to salvage the marriage by generous forgiveness and, in some cases, by his great attention to the giving of more affective and effective love. It would be destructive of hope to teach that an act of adultery dissolves the marriage bond, because marriage would then no longer reflect the covenant of God with mankind. Even after greater sins than adultery, God preserves and re-establishes the covenant by forgiveness and reconciliation.

The questions posed here are quite different: What can the Church impose under grave sanction on the abandoned spouse whose marriage is thoroughly destroyed and dissolved? Must this person remain celibate all his/her life even when it becomes evident that it is psychologically more harmful to the person and to others than a new marriage? The question is not whether the Church can dissolve a God-sanctioned marriage, but whether, after the total destruction of the reality of marriage (not just after a sin of adultery), the bond of marriage in its contractual reality does absolutely preclude a second marriage.

---

[1] Denzinger-Schönmetzer, *Enchiridion symbolorum,* 1807.

Biblical scholars generally agree that they cannot prove either thesis with absolute certainty; however, many scholars of all Churches are strongly inclined to think that in this case also, the Bible as a whole calls for a morality which serves the well-being of persons. What could have been the best solution for all persons involved at a certain period of history need not necessarily be the most appropriate solution for a totally different social and cultural context. A study in depth is now going on in the form of a painstaking research as to what constitutes the total tradition of the Church in both the East and the West, and serious reflection about the possible consequences of various theoretically possible solutions. All Christians should show concern by praying that the Church may arrive at a right solution for millions of people who today find themselves in such difficult situations.

Evidently, the Church cannot fall short of her duty to promote the stability of marriage in absolute fidelity to divine teaching and in readiness to forgive generously. But when all such efforts have been exhausted, the Church has to face the question of showing mercy to those who are divorced or forever abandoned and who, in spite of all their good will, cannot live in celibacy. Is it not possible for the Catholic Church to adopt in a circumspect way a praxis which has been widespread in the East, at least since the second century, and which can be proved to have been in force at least sporadically in the Latin Church until the twelfth century? I have no ready answer to the question. However I consider it a sign of hope that moralists and pastors are losing sleep thinking about the problem, while in compassion and prayer they seek God's will.

As in a number of previous publications, I am more directly concerned here with those persons whose first marriage has failed and are now living in a second canonically invalid marriage. I am referring specifically to a second marriage that is a stable and humanly-speaking harmonious union. Should we try to separate such people knowing all the while that this would do great harm to them and to their children? Why can we not give absolution and admit to the Eucharist those who responsibly cannot separate and who, in conscience, are convinced that God does not impose on them the hazardous effort of living together as "brother and sister" when this might entail greater moral danger? Only callous rigorists settle the question with a simple response: "After all these people are sinners and so have no right to be admitted to the sacraments." One may ask: who are the greater sinners, the self-righteous rigorists who look down on the "unclean", or these people who are sorry for their past failures and are now searching truly for God's will?

Many pastors do sympathize with such couples but they respond in a way that seems to divorce the "sacramental system" from the proclamation of God's mercy. They say: "Of course, you should not doubt that God, in His infinite mercy, forgives you; your repentance for the sins of the past and your sincere good will show that His grace has reached you, but you cannot expect the Church to give this assurance through the sacrament of reconciliation and the partaking of the Eucharist." No doubt, this attitude is a great step forward compared to that rigorism which simply condemned these people outright and deprived them of any hope without qualm of conscience.

While the Church wrestles with the problem of whether or not she could and should allow remarriage for those abandoned spouses who have no hope of reviving the previous marriage and cannot live in celibacy without great moral hazards, we should at least apply the "internum forum solutions" to those who are living harmoniously in a second marriage and cannot be advised to separate. In the numerous cases in which the previous marriage was most probably never made in heaven, the existing harmonious marriage should enjoy the *"favor iuris";* this means that pastors should be warned not to tear asunder what most probably has the blessing of God. In this age when it is so difficult to live a lonely life, should not the fundamental right to marry prevail against a slight probability that the previous marriage was valid? At any rate, if people come to us in all sincerity and good will, we must model our conduct on that of Christ: "All that the Father gives Me will come to Me, and the man who comes to Me I will never turn away" (Jn 6:37).

The Church must be a true sacrament of Christ, and her sacramental practice must manifest her fidelity to Christ's mercy.

There must be no dichotomy between the proclamation of the message of salvation and the sacramental life of the Church. Faced with people of good will, the decisive question cannot be whether their marriage situation can be settled according to canon law but rather according to the principles so classically stated by St. Augustine: "God does not impose impossible things, but by giving his command, he admonishes you to do what you can and to pray for what you cannot do." [1]

The Church of the merciful Samaritan must forcefully contradict the pharisaical attitude of the spouse who, considering himself innocent, would like to consider his marriage non-existent because of an act of adultery on the part of his spouse. It is incumbent on the Church to convert the faithful from loveless judging to merciful reconciliation. She also has to see that her canon law, her explanation of moral principles and the sacramental practice all manifest Christ's basic mission, His coming to heal the contrite. As far as I can see, progress has been made in this direction of blending the call to fidelity with mercy and compassion. The Church is thus becoming more visibly a sacrament of hope.

The growth of this evangelical attitude in the Church is a sign of hope particularly for the evangelization of people in those cultures where Western canon law and casuistry are totally alien and alienating. The same is true with respect to coloured people in countries such as the United States. Slave-owners formerly made it impossible for their slaves to have stable marriages. If as priests we judge the coloured who are living harmoniously in a second stable marriage according to the dictates of canon law and not according to their own good will, we incriminate ourselves by becoming the accomplices of those who first ruined their family life.

Among many of the African tribes the concept of marriage differs considerably from that of our European and American tradition. While with us marital consent and subsequent physical union constitute together the whole reality of marriage, most African peoples regard marriage more as a developing reality to

---

[1] *De natura et gratia,* cap. 43, CSEL 60, 270.

be finalized and solemnized only at a later date. They have their own ideas about priorities and moral concepts. When young people come to live together, it is a matter of social responsibility. They have a sincere intention of marriage; they look forward to a lasting covenant. But there is a period of time during which not only the two spouses but also the two families are involved in observing whether or not it will work out as a stable and happy union. It is only after a serious effort and often after the first child has been born that the tentative partnership becomes an irrevocable marriage. The decisive part of the dowry is handed over and the customary ceremonies take place attesting to the final commitment not only of the two spouses but also of the two clans involved in this marital pact.

To my knowledge, missionaries react to the custom by advising Christians that the canonical celebration of the sacrament should coincide with the tribal finalization. In the meantime, however, the young couple looking forward to finalization of their marriage bond are excluded from the sacramental life of the Church at a time when they particularly need it. It hurts them if the practice, deeply rooted in their whole tradition and culture, is regarded as concubinage or living in a proximate occasion of sin. Exclusion from the sacraments and the whole system of discrimination has had no noticeable impact on the practice; it has failed to bring about any change in their customs and serves only as a permanent cause of alienation from the Church.

Two years ago I wrote an article in *Christus* entitled: "Contestation missionaire de la morale"; the article is now a chapter of my book *Theology of Protest* under the title of "The Missionary Dimension of Protest". This article inspired a number of bishops to reconsider their policy. For example, in one diocese the following changes were made: the young couple would no longer be excluded from the sacraments provided the following conditions were met: (1) if at the time they came together, they announced the fact to the catechist or to the pastor; (2) if, by affixing their signature to an official document, they expressed their serious intention to finalize the marriage at the proper time, provided there were no grave obstacles; (3) if, in the meantime, they received instruction on how to live a Christian married life and learn to grow in faith and love, praying together. Instead of alienating couples, this new approach helps to make this period a kind of novitiate or something similar to temporary vows during the first years of religious life. This is the African way; and under present circumstances such may well be the only way to bring hope to them, at least until cultural change makes possible a more ideal regulation.

Pastoral mercy can and should give rise to hope and we need to free ourselves from a judging attitude that betrays our lack of knowledge about man and his behaviour and reflects a static view of morality. Life is growth and as such bears the mark of hope. Therefore, we must never try to impose an abstract ideal on people; rather we should help them orient themselves definitively towards the ideal goal while searching humbly, patiently and courageously for the next possible step in the right direction. Furthermore, knowledge of man's social nature will not permit us to separate individual effort from social reform.

Both in the Church and in the world, only a constant and radical conversion striving towards a synthesis of justice and mercy with personal responsibility and social reform can free mankind from the great temptation of despair and from the many failures to which a lack of hope gives rise.

Chapter 17

THE COURAGE TO BE

Some time ago, I had the privilege of meeting one of those humble saints whose thoughts were far removed from any dream of canonization by herself or others. The young lady lived with a very refractory husband for seven and half years. He held four doctorates but in no way could his intellectual ability compensate for his total heartlessness as a husband. He was insensitive to the point of complete sexual impotence. Still the young woman remained supremely confident that in time she would be able to help him overcome his psychological hurdles. But that hope gradually faded away. She had no trouble obtaining a marriage annulment in the civil courts. When I met her, she had been waiting four years for a similar decision on the part of the ecclesiastical tribunal. She had submitted to the required medical examination to ascertain whether or not her hymen had been perforated; it was found to be intact. The ecclesiastical annulment was finally granted.

As her spiritual guide I found it difficult to contain my own feelings of anger and indignation. Her personal stamina and fortitude had carried her through the ordeal without a nervous collapse. In fact, she was profoundly grateful for the privilege of living with her dear parents, brothers and sisters again. She felt that the Church's formalism was indeed regrettable but she retained peace of mind in the face of the most trying circumstances. The only frustration she ever voiced was: why could she not pursue her work helping other people? For many years she had devoted the best of her energies to assisting exceptional children; they were an object of great concern to her and she found the work rewarding. She sensed strongly that these children were capable of great affection and gratitude.

I learned a great deal from counselling such a person; she led me to a deeper appreciation of the jarring passage in the Epistle to the Hebrews: Christ "learned obedience in the school of suffering, and, once perfected, became the source of eternal salvation for all who obey Him" (Heb 5:8). It is evident that in this context, obedience means the constant acceptance of any personal mission by entrusting ourselves to Christ in faith so that He can manifest the full depth of His love. He is the Divine Master of unselfish love for all who consent to follow Him.

As long as we oscillate between optimism and pessimism, we cannot grasp completely the uniqueness of Christian hope; this humble lady exemplified the courage of being Christian in its fullest sense. What sustained her through the many years of constant thwarting and thanklessness was her faith in the Paschal Mystery with its treasure of joy that inspired courage to accept suffering in union with Christ. Her faith reflected the redemptive power of love and the sense of dedication needed to serve the severely handicapped. She accepted the challenges of life in a spirit of thanksgiving.

When we are faced with such biographies, it becomes evident that all optimistic metaphysical systems ring empty and superficial. He who approaches life with the simple enthusiastic expectation that "everything will be all right" is ill-prepared to confront life in its reality. The day will come when all illusions will collapse and there will then be nothing but scorching bitterness. Today's pessimism arises from the superficial optimism that marked the world of yesterday. People tended to expect much more from the world than it could offer, or occasionally they expected too little of it. Their expectations and hopes were lacking in depth and they consequently were traumatized when they had to go on living in the midst of so many upsets and disillusionments.

Pessimism turns out to be the most deceitful of all doctrines; it is afraid of suffering. It flees from the battlefield of life and betrays its deepest meaning. Pessimism renounces the fullness of life because it lacks the courage to be. The pessimist is wanting in the resoluteness to face reality in depth and to probe all its possibilities, that is, he refuses to learn love in the school of suffering. To know that life brings pain and freely to accept suffering as part of life's total meaning, to understand the significance of suffering not so much as an abstraction as by the courage to be authentically Christian, to come to the actualization of the best of oneself in the midst of trials and frustration — this is what Chritsian hope does and alone can do.

It is not so much suffering itself as an apparent "senselessness" that makes it so unbearable to many. Man can bear up under the most terrible sufferings if he discovers some deep meaning in them. This presupposes that man yearns for a total grasp of the significance of life although he may come to this knowledge only gradually and through growing pains. The total meaning of suffering is love that hopes, and hope that discovers gradually the dimensions of true love.

The courage to be and to find one's true self in the midst of suffering — not only in spite of it but especially by confronting it — manifests the full depth of human freedom. Freedom comes into its own only when it accepts the greatest challenges in life and love. To seek a life on earth in which there will be no more suffering and no more frustration is a coward's way of escaping from freedom's choice and its highest dignity. Freedom grows with our courageous "yes" to the real conditions of life and in full awareness of the complexity of the present situation including its many possibilities and limitations.

Anyone who dares to face his own need for purification knows that suffering can offer the greatest opportunity for freedom. I refer specifically to those sufferings which appear to be the price for justice and peace; they are a test of unselfish love and fidelity in the school of the Divine Master. Enjoying such a freedom, a person can endure suffering not only without being hurt but even looking on it as a royal path to still greater freedom because he has already opted for its saving meaning.

L

The first beatitude reminds us of the strength that comes from the acceptance of suffering: "How blest are those who know that they are poor" (Mt 5:3). Underpinning this beatitude is the awareness that all good gifts come from God. Included in this notion of poverty is the courage to face one's own unworthiness with trust that God is infinitely good to those who are simple-hearted and humble; he grants them a share of his kingdom.

The high-mettled acceptance of purifying sufferings betokens a sincere yearning to experience the blessedness of those "whose hearts are pure" (Mt 5:8). It is the courage to be while sensing the need to become; it implies the resoluteness to come to the full integration of one's personality by accepting the daily need of further purification and conversion. It is the courage of a sinner to be a son of God knowing full well that one can only be so because of God's active mercy and patience: "You must endure it as discipline: God is treating you as sons. Can anyone be a son, who is not disciplined by his father? If you escape the discipline in which all sons share, you must be bastards and no true sons" (Heb 12:7-8). The courage to be a son comes only from God's gracious and undeserved action of purification opening the heart and mind in an existential way to the most hidden beatitude: "How blest are the sorrowful; they shall find consolation" (Mt 5:4).

Sin results in the most dangerous and depressing kind of frustration. It has about it all the offensive odour of despair. The idle and self-centred regrets that follow sin strangle the creative energies of hope. They confine man more securely than ever in the helplessness of an imprisoned selfish ego. Sorrow in Christ makes possible a new opening to God, neighbour and true self. Sorrow involves a new acceptance of oneself and one's sufferings. It brings man's failures into the saving love and light of Christ. It reveals an acceptance of suffering in which the power of the Paschal Mystery is operative.

The acceptance of oneself with all one's limitations and failures is not possible without profound suffering, but it is a healing experience. It is precisely sorrow in Christ that leads to a new redemptive acceptance of oneself. It opens up new horizons of being and leads to a more out-going form of existence. Redemptive suffering with self-acceptance is a condition for the redemptive meaning of all the sufferings which a person is likely to encounter on his way towards self-realization in community.

Self-acceptance is a prelude to responsibility, to the courage to bear along with one's own burden a part of the burden of one's neighbour. It prepares us to be increasingly grateful towards those who bear a part of our own burden.

Sorrow in Christ also frees us from self-pity. It means a sharing in the suffering of the One who came to bear the burdens of all. In the blessed sorrow of a contrite heart, the eyes are opened to the horrifying dimensions of sin as an injustice to God's love and as an obstacle to the salvation of the world. The contrite sinner realizes that each sin is a source of dangerous environmental pollution in which many will have to suffer unless he himself, by suffering, purifies his heart in order to become a source of salvation in his immmediate surroundings. But this profound suffering is very much akin to the pangs of childbirth which portend the hope of a new life. It is the prologue to a creative change towards openness in justice and love.

"How blest are you who weep now; you shall laugh" (Lk 6:21). Blessed are those who opt for purifying suffering instead of the oppressive frustration of self-pity and anger. Blessed are those who, through faith and hope, opt for a right understanding of life while facing its vexations. They will increasingly display the courage to be and the courage to become. They will experience the joy associated with the fullness of a life continually unfolding itself.

Chapter 18

HOPE AT ITS SOURCE

In the midst of all his frailties and failures, what constitutes the fountainhead of man's hope? There are many fountains and sources but not all furnish clear water.

Work as an expression of the creative self especially when performed in the service of humanity is one means of self-realization. It brings joy and increases a healthy self-trust. But if man works only for self-actualization or devotes all his energies to, and places all his trust in work, then with each failure his confidence will waver and become subject to re-examination.

There is joy and expectation in study and reflection, in scientific inquiry, especially in the experience of sharing in the process itself and in the results of research. They can contribute greatly to the enrichment of life, but all too often the fragmentation characteristic of modern science and the lag in the implementation of the findings constitute a source of frustration.

Reflection, meditation and dialogue about the great questions of life, faith and revelation serve to undergird life and hope. They demand depth of thought but we should not tarry on the abstract level where God remains an "it"; the fact that research and speculation so often remain on a theoretical plane can become an insurmountable obstacle to faith in a living God. Theory can degenerate into futile disputes, as it has in the past in the case of theological schools and separated churches. Even an interior contemplation that pursues only peace of mind cannot totally direct man to God in hope and faith.

With hope, man turns to his innermost depth where being at home means "being with" and an "outgoing existence"; it is there that man entrusts himself to God. This is the very heart of the process of prayer. Hope attains maturity in adoring love of God and in active love of fellowman provided this love is rooted in God and leads to a deeper awareness of the presence of God.

Man's own capacities, energies and achievements can be a source of natural optimism but one that is always threatened by misgivings and failings. The more man reaches out towards maturity and the courage to be, the more he becomes aware of his own limitations; this helps create a healthy insecurity in him. There is no other path for the man-come-of-age than this "holy insecurity". It is a life trustfully lived in the presence of God, who alone can give to a frail creature the courage to be and to become in the midst of human insecurity. It means a total reliance on God after we have learned the wholesome way of self-doubt and distrust of the world in so far as this world does not place all its confidence in God.

In prayer, life and hope are at their source, whether it be the prayer of praise and thanksgiving, the prayer of sorrow or the prayer of petition. Thanksgiving brings many to the blessed consciousness that good things are more than material realities because they come from God. They are signs of God's loving presence and care, a constant appeal to us to entrust ourselves to Him and to radiate hope by the utilization of His gifts as signs of the hoped-for solidarity of all men in God. We have referred earlier to the hopeful character of the prayer of sorrow which allows even the greatest sinner to have the courage to be, while he experiences the dawning of a creative transformation.

The prayer of petition reflects hope to the extent that it expresses or increases absolute trust and confidence in God. We are assured by faith that God will grant us whatever we ask in the name of Jesus, that is, increase in wisdom and love, light and fellowship in the Holy Spirit. In the prayer of petition the believer knows that God will grant him more than he is asking for, and he is prepared to receive whatever comes unexpectedly with that same confidence and trust. "God is a generous giver who neither refuses nor reproaches anyone. Man must ask in faith, without a doubt in mind; for the doubter is like a heaving sea ruffled by the wind" (James 1:5-6).

The Lord Himself tells us exactly what we should long and hope for; He does so in the Our Father. Our first prayerful demand in hope pertains to the courage to live as children of the one God and Father. It calls for that courage to believe whole-heartedly that in Christ we not only bear the name of children, but even on earth we can hope to honour the name of the one Father by promoting the brotherhood of men. It implies a resoluteness to do so patiently, knowing full well that final and complete manifestation awaits the end of history.

Prayer introduces us to the salvific tension between the "already" and the "not yet", thus turning us into untiring pilgrims. It does not allow us to dream of a perfect anticipation of the heavenly mode of dwelling in God's love nor does it allow us to look lazily at the skies. When our prayer is sincere, we set out with God's grace towards the heavenly way of doing God's will, that is, in a spirit of praise and thanksgiving and in full solidarity with all of God's children and his creation.

When we kneel before God in prayer we learn that it is not permissible to long and hope merely for one's own bread; prayer extends our hope to all men, so that they may learn to share their bread, co-ordinate their skills and utilize their organizational talents to feed all men. Before God we realize that men crave not only for money and nourishment for their body. To eat our bread together means acknowledging effectively the dignity and freedom of all men and allowing them an active part, a real co-responsibility in economic, cultural, political and international life.

When praying for our own needs, we realize more and more how the sharing of our daily bread takes place at the common table of life. In partaking together of the word of God and of the Eucharistic Bread, we realize that we can effectively hope for the heavenly banquet only in that solidarity of hope with which our whole life says "Our Father". It is through prayer that we come to an ever fuller realization of how we should hope for peace and reconciliation. We are "sacred liars", i.e., we are uttering unholy lies using sacred words when we hope for the gift of shalom without evincing any willingness to be peacemakers. It is through prayer that we come to the existential understanding that we cannot escape the dark powers in our own heart and our environment unless we commit ourselves simultaneously to the purification of our own self and to the building up of a divine *milieu* of goodness, kindness, sincerity, purity and justice.

Prayer is hope in operation because it is hope at the very source of all creative and redemptive action. Being at home in God's loving design means being a part of His promises for the world. Thus we become bridges of hope capable of spanning the gap between faith and life. If our hope in prayer is truly Christian, the whole world in us, with us and through us, attains the source of its hope, since we hope and pray for the well-being and salvation of the whole world.

Prayer is hope at its source only if it follows the prophetic tradition that excludes any dichotomy between religion and life, between faith and hope, between love of God and love of neighbour. Formalism is one of the greatest threats to prayer and hope. Of course, some structure is needed for our common celebrations and prayer, but there must always be room for spontaneity and creativity. The whole system of prayer must allow freedom to the Spirit who renews the face of the earth.

Prayer is hope in action only if it thoroughly follows the Word Incarnate, and therefore in no way inclines towards a Hellenistic concept of contemplation which tries to escape reality and commitment to the visible world. The prayer of active hope makes man a sharer of God's Sabbath-repose that gives life, peace and direction to His creative presence in the world.

Prophetic prayer arises from experiencing solidarity with sufferers, the poor, the discriminated-against, the oppressed; it offers this vital solidarity to God in Jesus Christ to be strengthened and deepened. Thus does hope at its very source make the believer an ever more effective sign, a "sacrament" of hope for the world. The more hope remains at its source through a genuine prophetic prayer, the more the messengers of hope can bring a sense of wholeness to life, integrate the expectation of the final coming of the Lord and His coming in daily events, and synthesize hope for "the new earth and the new heaven" with a commitment to a better world in which man can live while on earth.

As far as we men are concerned, hope at its source gives God freedom to be everything in all things. In prayer we commit ourselves in trust to God, granting Him a free hand to remove all obstacles to the fulfilment of His promises.

Hope in action, an active trust that fosters hope in our neighbours and in the world around us, is prayer whenever two are gathered in the name of Christ. In full awareness, they consent in word and in deed to that solidarity which is the sign that they are at the source of hope in God.

Illiterate Russian peasants have communicated this truth to me in a most forceful and hope-inspiring way. When after the battle of Stalingrad in an effort to escape captivity along with sixteen gravely wounded and sick men I arrived alone at the house of a poor Russian family, we were taken in as cordially as if these people had received Christ Himself. The family sheltered us in spite of the grave dangers involved; the highway on which the Russian army kept moving back and forth was very near.

These poor Russians fed the hungry men and cared for them through the night. This was the most secular language about God but His name was not mentioned. Before leaving I asked what could have motivated them to such a courageous manifestation of love to enemies of their country. The mother of the household replied with the greatest simplicity: "We have four of our sons in the Russian army and each day we pray that God will bring them home safe and sound. How could we go on praying if today we had overlooked the fact that your mother,

177

your father and your friends are praying to the same God for the very same thing?" This is the prayer of hope in action.

Forms of prayer or better still, "prayers" that do not bear fruit for the life of the world are not truly "hope at its source"; rather they are expressions of man's self-made religion. Similarly, action that does not strengthen an awareness of God's presence in the world is not hope coming from its source. It may even lead away from Him who alone is the hope of the world.

The fast-growing House of Prayer movement aims at a prophetic synthesis, the integration of prayer and life, hope at its source and hope in action, the courage to be in the world trusting in God and the confidence that we are bringing hope closer to the world when we turn totally to God.